Smuaintean fo Éiseabhal

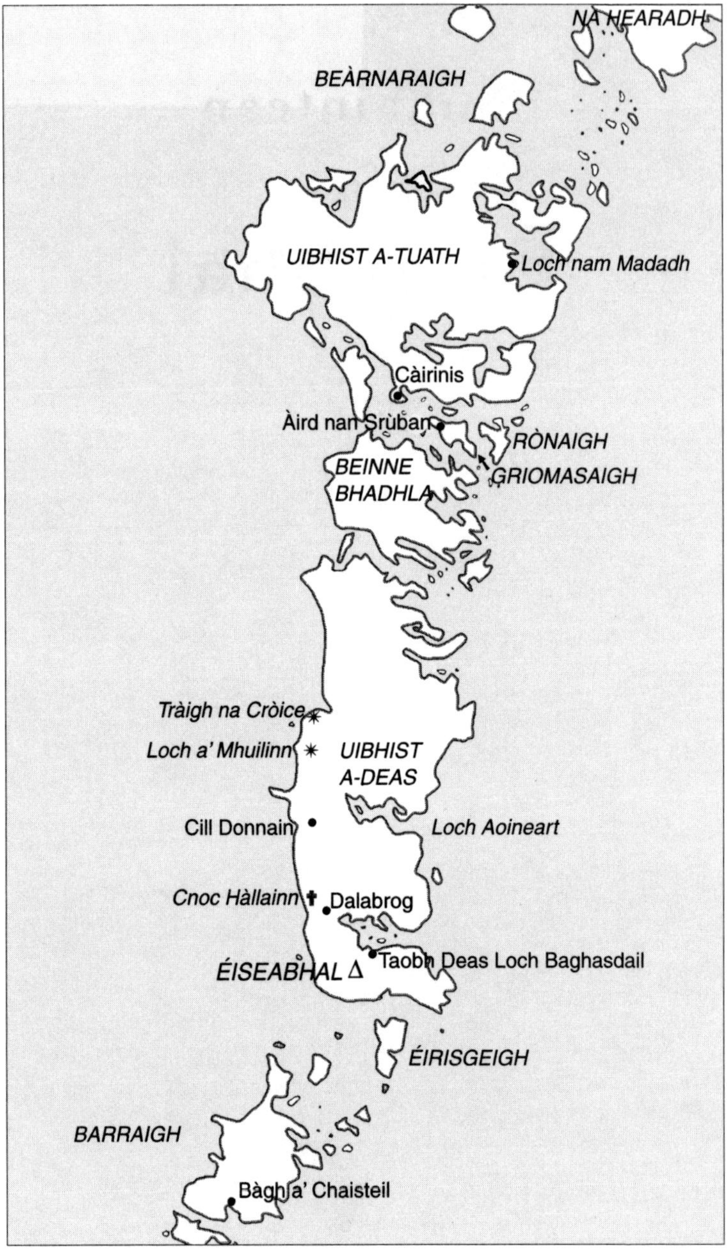
NA HEARADH
BEÀRNARAIGH
UIBHIST A-TUATH
Loch nam Madadh
Càirinis
Àird nan Srùban
RÒNAIGH
BEINNE
BHADHLA
GRIOMASAIGH
Tràigh na Cròice
Loch a' Mhuilinn
UIBHIST
A-DEAS
Cill Donnain
Loch Aoineart
Cnoc Hàllainn
Dalabrog
ÉISEABHAL
Taobh Deas Loch Baghasdail
ÉIRISGEIGH
BARRAIGH
Bàgh a' Chaisteil

Smuaintean fo Éiseabhal

Thoughts under Easaval

le
Dòmhnall Aonghais Bhàin
(Donald MacDonald)

edited by
Ronald Black

Birlinn

First published in 2000 by
Birlinn Limited
8 Canongate Venture
5 New Street
Edinburgh
EH8 8BH

http://www.birlinn.co.uk

ISBN 1 84158 108 9

British Library Cataloguing-in-Publication Data
A catalogue record for this book is available
from the British Library

Typeset in Horley Old Style by
Edderston Book Design, Peebles
Printed and bound by
Creative Print and Design, Ebbw Vale

Clàr-Innse / Contents

Na Dàin: *Poems with English Translation*

Na Dàin: *Poems without English Translation*

Roimh-Ràdha

Aonghas Pàdraig Caimbeul

Dòmhnall Aonghais Bhàin. Crom, anns na dungarees. Dhà no trì fhàdan mònadh fo achlais, 's e a-nis air siubhal: 's nach ann aige a tha na deagh chompanaich, shìos an-sin ann a Hàllainn. M' athair fhìn nam measg. Calum, bràthair Shomhairle. Iain mac Dhòmhnaill 'ic Iain Bhàin. Seonaidh Roidein. Mìle Dòmhnall eile. Flòraidh neo dhà: Gaidhil na ficheadamh linn. 'S na naoidheamh linn deug. 'S na h-ochdamh linn deug, 's air ais.

Agus seo sinn a-nis, air fhàgail. Ann an linn na h-eadar-lìn. Am bàrd mu dheireadh, anns an taigh-tughaidh mu dheireadh, air falbh, 's an còrr againn ag obair dha *Oilthigh na Gaidhealtachd*, a' taomadh às *free verse* a shadadh mo sheanair dhan bhin. Nam biodh bin air a bhith aige.

Oir bhuineadh Dòmhnall Aonghais Bhàin dhan t-seann nòs: an nòs far an robh ceangal mòr eadar briathran agus fuaim: far an robh *cluain* is *cuan* is *snuadh*, is *gnùis* is *driùchd* is *smùr* a' bualadh ann am Mac-alla an Dùin, mar chanadh an Clàrsair Dall. Ach thàinig Eliot is Pound nach tàinig, 's thug sinne bha òg 's nach do dh'èist riamh ri Seonaidh mac Dhòmhnaill 'ic Iain Bhàin soraidh slàn ri *iar* is *sian* is *ciar*. Dh'fhalbh sinn *free-wheeling*, 's dh'fhàg sinn na bodaich bhochd air ar cùlaibh.

'S thàinig a' Hydro-Electric – eil cuimhn' agaibh? Cassius Clay agus Sonny Liston agus Floyd Paterson agus Dà Cheathramh agus Fonn. Chaidh Èirdsidh Grannd a Ghlaschu, 's e dol iomrall 's dol air chall. The noise was just like thunder, dear. 'S thàinig Niall á Afraga is thug e muncaidh dhachaigh leis. 'S dh'fhalbh Yuri Gagarin, 's thàinig na Beatles. Agus an telly: na h-Òganaich! Poldark! Ironside! Crann Tàra! Last of the Summer Wine! Boys from the Blackstuff! Telefios!

Hud! Dè feum a bh' againne air bàrdachd? Nach robh an *Daily Record* a h-uile latha ann am Bùth Ailean, agus a' *West Highland Free Press* gach seachdain air bhan Lovat. Weren't we all speaking English, a bhalaich. Slàint'. And isn't this the age of information technology, 'ille? E-mail dot com slash forward BBC dot slash. Bàrdachd? Nam biodh fhios agad, 'ille. Hee-haw MacCodrum. Clann 'Ic Mhuirich? Phwah!

'S am measg a' ghòraiche bha sin, chum Dòmhnall Aonghais Bhàin a' dol. Anns na dungarees. Anns an taigh-tughaidh. Leis fhèin. Gun taic bho Oilthigh. Gun ghrant bhon Scottish Arts Council. Gun feum air Pròiseact nan Ealain. Gun BMW aig ceann an taighe. Fhads a bha na bàird ùr (mi fhìn nam measg) a' cur a-mach *publicity*, gar moladh fhèin, bha Dòmhnall air Èiseabhal, ag èisteachd ri na h-eòin, a' seinn na eanchainn am measg nan slàn-lusan 's nan cluarain. Mo bheannachd air. Air irisileachd 's air a choibhneas. Air a ghràdh airson Uibhist, nàdarach agus daonnda. Airson a dhìlseachd agus airson cumail ri na seann dòighean làidir fallain. Gun a leigeil air falbh air dholaidh, mar a bha an còrr againn a' dèanamh. *Fraoch* a' ruith ri *raon*, 's an uair sin *raon* a' ruith ri *taobh*. Chan eil iongnadh gun robh e tric a' smaointinn nach robh duine beò a' leughadh na bha e a' sgrìobhadh. Nach robh e ann an Gàidhlig? Ann an Gàidhlig an latha dè? Mu bhòidhchead Èiseabhail? A-rithist. Nach robh cus obrach ann dhuinn a leughadh, is Eòrpa, le fo-thiotalan, air an teilidh? Amarusso aig Ibrox fhads a bha Dòmhnall am Bàgh Hartabhagh.

Ach thàinig an latha, agus seo e: mu dheireadh thall, cruinneachadh ceart dhe a chuid bhàrdachd: na briathran 's na rannan, na smuaintean 's na beachdan, na h-ìomhaighean 's na fuaimean. Na fuaimean gu sònraichte: na fuaimreagan cho cumanta 's cho bunaiteach: aithris iad a-mach le blas ceann a-deas Uibhist a-Deas 's gheibh thu iad mar bu chòir:

Èiseabhal st**ù**cach nan **ù**r-bhl**à**th 's nan cl**ua**n
'S nan **ai**bhnichean si**ù**bhlach 's an c**ù**rsa gu c**ua**n,
Nan g**o**rm-ghl**ai**cean fl**ù**rach tha **ù**rail 'nan sn**ua**dh —
'S tha 'n t-s**ò**bhrag 's an cl**ua**ran a' f**à**s ann.

Chòrd sin le Dòmhnall – na fuaimean fhèin. Mar a chòrd iad le Dòmhnall Ruadh Phàislig agus Dòmhnall Iain Dhonnchaidh agus Dòmhnall Ailean Dhòmhnaill na Bainich agus le gach bàrd a rugar riamh. Ach feumaidh mi seo a ràdh cuideachd: nach bu chòir do bhàrd sam bith a bhith na phrìosanach gu na fuaimean sin. Bu chòir dha gach facal a bhith fo uachdranais a' bhàird, 's chan ann air a chaochladh. Uaireannan, ann am bàrdachd Dhòmhnaill, bha cus cumhachd aig na fuaimean. 'S nuair a thachras sin, saoilidh mi gu bheil na faireachdainnean, agus neart na h-aigne agus spiorad na bàrdachd, air am mùchadh: tha e mar gum biodh na fuaimean fhèin a' bàthadh nam briathran. 'S nuair a thachras sin, chan e bàrdachd a th' agad ach buillean.

Ach cha b'e coire Dhòmhnaill a bha sin na bu mhotha, ach coire an rud ris an can sinn uile *an siostam*. A Dhia nan gràis, nach robh sinn uile air ar murt agus air ar marbhadh leis an t-seòrsa teagaisg a bha dol san fhicheadamh linn – an rud a fhuair Dòmhnall san sgoil, agus an dearbh rud a fhuair mise: ìompaireachdas, ann an litreachas is eile, a' dol eadar Sgoil Ghearraidh na Mònadh ann an Uibhist agus Sgoil Ghearraidh na Mònadh anns na h-Innsean. Dè fhuair sinn uile, eadar Baghasdal agus Bombay, ach Wordsworth, agus Kipling, agus Keats agus Shelley:

Thou still unravished bride of quietness,
Thou foster-child of silence and slow time,
Sylvan historian, who canst thus express

A flowery tale more sweetly than our rhyme:
What leaf-fringed legend haunts about thy shape
Of deities or mortals, or of both,
In Tempe or the dales of Arcady?
What men or gods are these? What maidens loth?
What mad pursuit? What struggle to escape?
What pipes and timbrels? What wild ecstasy?

Cha robh e dèanamh ciall dhomh an uair sin, 's mi beag anns an sgoil an Uibhist. 'S chan eil e dèanamh ciall dhomh fhathast.

B'e a' mhìorbhail, tha mi cinnteach, gun d'fhuair duin' againn thairis air ar cuid foghlaim. Gun do thionndaidh duin' againn gu bàrdachd idir. S dòcha, ri linn sin, nach eil iongnadh sam bith gun do thionndaidh Dòmhnall Aonghais Bhàin air ais chun an t-seann nòs agus cuid againn chun an dearbh chaochladh, chun an nòs ùr. Bha sàbhailteachd, mas fhìor, ann an aon nòs agus saorsa, mas fhìor, anns an nòs eile. Air ar glacadh eadar John Masefield agus Sandy Shaw. Like a puppet on a string. Ach beag an t-saorsa bha anns an fhear a bha sàbhailte, agus beag sàbhailteachd a bha anns an fhear a bha saorsanachail. 'S dè a-nis?

Se an obair a-nis, tha mi creidsinn, saorsa fhaighinn bho gach slabhraidh. A bhith anns an taigh-tughaidh, s dòcha, ach le compiutar. A bhith am measg nan dot coms, ach le greim Dhòmhnaill Aonghais Bhàin air na fuaimreagan 's an rannaidheachd. 'S chan eil a leithid cho furasta a dhèanamh 's a tha e ri ràdh. Doimhneachd ann, mar treas-fàd na trèisgeir. Sìos dhan bhoglaich leibh far eil e fliuch agus doirbh – ach abair na caorain a gheibh thu ás nuair thig an tiormachadh! An fheadhainn a their dhut teas agus solas lainnearach a' gheamhraidh.

A Dhòmhnaill, tha mi moiteil gun robh mi eòlach ort. Gun do bheannaich thu a' chlann bheag agam air taobh an stòbh an-uiridh. Am *Modern Mistress* a tha Ailig ag ainmeachadh (td xxii). Agus eil fhios agad air a-seo, a Dhòmhnaill? B' fhiach e. B' fhiach. Eil thu 'g èisteachd? Tha nighean bheag agamsa, agus chan eil i ach seachd agus tuigidh i gach facal a sgrìobh thu. 'S chan e mhàin gum bheil i gan tuigsinn, ach tha i gan creidsinn, oir tha eòlas aicese cuideachd air gràdh. Buinidh i dhan 21st century, ach tha i gad thoirt-sa leat air a gualainn. Bidh an leabhar seo na màileid, dot com ann no às.

Mo bheannachd oirre. Agus air Raghnall agus an fheadhainn eile a chuir an leabhar seo a-mach air a' mhòintich. Ach gu h-àraid ort fhèin, a Dhòmhnaill. Gu h-àraid ort fhèin. A-nis: dè mu dheidhinn deagh chupa tì?

Fearann Dòmhnaill, An t-Eilean Sgitheanach
An t-Ògmhios 2000

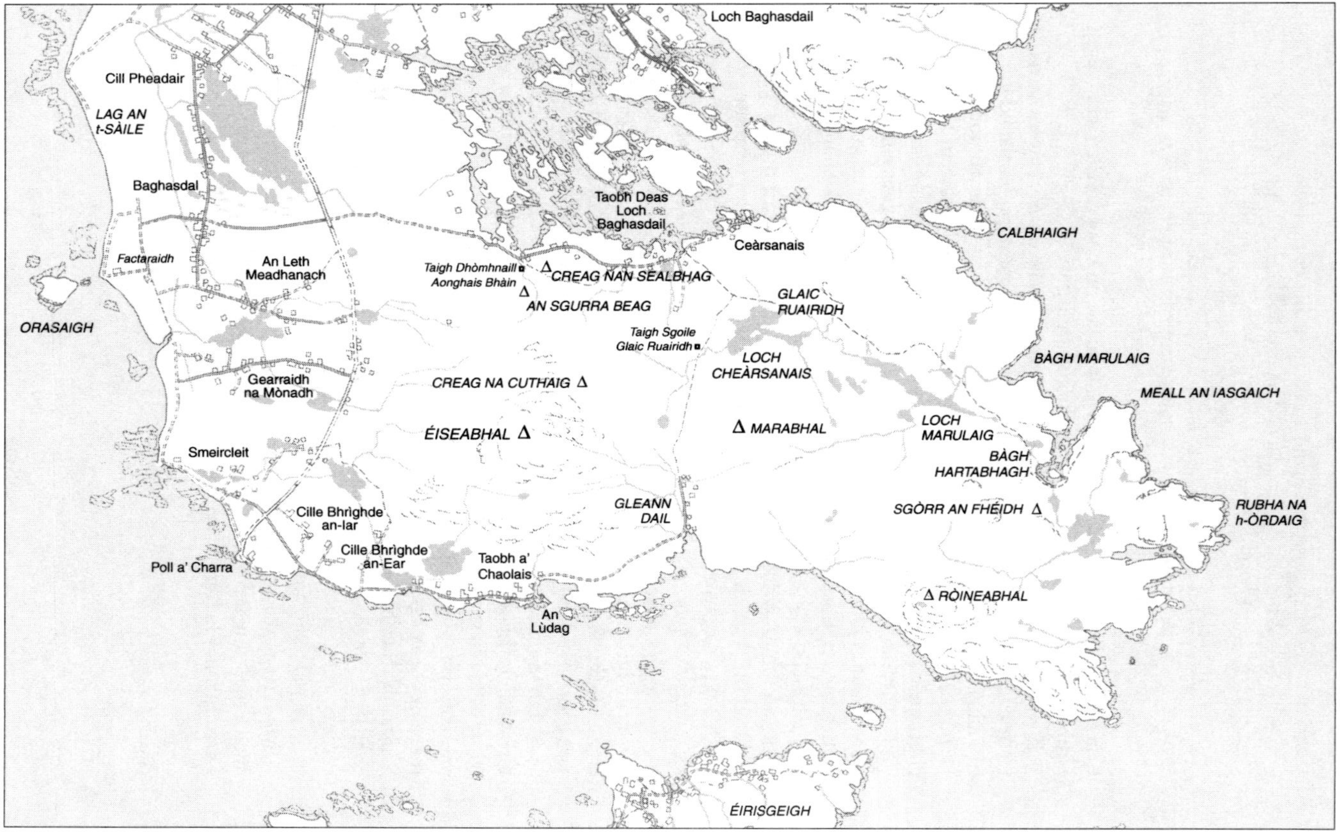
Loch Baghasdail
Cill Pheadair
LAG AN t-SÀILE
Baghasdal
Factaraidh
ORASAIGH
An Leth Meadhanach
Gearraidh na Mònadh
Smeircleit
Poll a' Charra
Cille Bhrìghde an-Iar
Cille Bhrìghde an-Ear
Taobh a' Chaolais
An Lùdag
Taigh Dhòmhnaill Aonghais Bhàin
CREAG NAN SEALBHAG
AN SGURRA BEAG
CREAG NA CUTHAIG
ÉISEABHAL
Taobh Deas Loch Baghasdail
Ceàrsanais
GLAIC RUAIRIDH
Taigh Sgoile Glaic Ruairidh
LOCH CHEÀRSANAIS
MARABHAL
GLEANN DAIL
CALBHAIGH
BÀGH MARULAIG
MEALL AN IASGAICH
LOCH MARULAIG
BÀGH HARTABHAGH
SGÒRR AN FHÉIDH
RUBHA NA h-ÒRDAIG
RÒINEABHAL
ÉIRISGEIGH

Introduction

Ronald Black

The making of this book began within weeks of Dòmhnall Aonghais Bhàin's death. I was asked by Mrs Jacqueline Marsh if I could help put together a few of his poems as a handout to accompany the exhibition of his life and work which is to open at Kildonan Museum in South Uist in July 2000. My answer was that it might be possible to do better than that. And thanks to the enthusiasm of Hugh Andrew of Birlinn, who last year published the ground-breaking *Voice of the Bard*, I was proved right.

Mrs Marsh and I set about gathering the poems. The more I read, the more Dòmhnall's work grew in my estimation. The trouble about it had always been its niceness. Ever since I first met Dòmhnall in the 1960s he had been pouring out a stream of little poems on the beauties of Uist and of womanhood. These tended to be repetitive and appeared regularly for many years in *The Stornoway Gazette* and *Am Pàipear*. The uneasy feeling that Dòmhnall could best be described as a 'naive poet' was compounded by the appearance in *The Voice of the Bard* of a poem in praise of Camilla Parker Bowles.

I was aware, however, of strengths in Dòmhnall's work which made him more than a naive poet. And as I read what we had gathered, I came across items that made him more even than a minor poet. An outstanding lovesong. Free-flowing, well-wrought lyricism. Elegantly-expressed thoughts on death and change. A very funny piece of township verse full of a quality otherwise foreign to his work – irony.

Then there was 'Mìosan na Bliadhna' (p. 44), which was apparently inspired by Longfellow (*Voice of the Bard* p. 9). I had long been attracted to this poem as a concept, but had found it curiously flawed in structure. Part of the problem I think was that experimental Gaelic verse requires sensitive typesetting of a kind scarcely possible in newspapers. For this *is* a truly experimental poem. Its 'flawed' structure, I now realised, was deliberate – the work of a man who knew exactly how traditional verse should be composed, but who had developed the confidence to break ancient rules and lifetime habits for the sake of furthering his art.

Finally I came to realise that Dòmhnall, the last of so many traditional poets from the area, had made himself the voice of the hills of Boisdale (*Baghasdal*, the Norsemen's 'Valley of the Bays'), if I may use the name in its older sense as the whole of that part of South Uist south of Loch Boisdale (see map opposite). I decided that my selection of poems should reflect this function. The focus and symbol of this *dùthchas* is the hill called Easaval (*Éiseabhal*) which rises up behind Dòmhnall's house. It is the highest summit in Boisdale. Dòmhnall never possessed a car or learned to drive, but he clearly walked every inch of the territory that he could reach from his home and loved it with an intensity which is quite unusual even for Gaelic verse. *Gach àit' anns an gluais sinn bidh e fuaight' ruinn le gaol*, he says (p. 36), "Every place in which we walk is made a part of us by love." When he published a series of his poems in *Gairm* in 1982 he chose for them the title 'Smuaintean fo Éiseabhal'. That, then, is now the title of this book.

Dòmhnall Aonghais Bhàin was the inheritor of a rich tradition of community verse, but this tradition died during his lifetime, leaving him as high and dry as the 'Old Lighthouse of Calvay' which serves as his *alter ego*. As I showed at p. xlv of *An Tuil*, his work may therefore be seen as one of a number of different responses to that situation by poets in various parts of the Gaelic-speaking world during the second half of the twentieth century.

> Angus Campbell, 'Am Puilean', did his best to re-invent the ceilidh-house tradition in more basic accommodation, but the idea got out of hand, fell foul of the church, and his little ceilidh-houses turned into the rural drinking-dens well known to the English-medium press in the 1960s as 'bothans'. Donald John MacDonald simplified the vocabulary of his hymns, which retained a public audience, while maintaining demanding standards in his secular verse, which became more personal. His uncle Donald Macintyre despaired of his work reaching anyone any more, and attempted to consign it to the flames. Donald Allan MacDonald ceased composing altogether and became that contradiction in terms, a dumb poet: as he did not write his material, his legacy is now full of gaps. Dòmhnall Aonghais Bhàin disseminates his work through the print media, but needs a little reassurance now and again that it is being read. Donald R Morrison does likewise, and is willing to write in English if requested; his substitute for oral memory is libraries, to which he regularly sends his work. Curiously, the change worked slightly to the advantage of poets who were not singers: Ian Paterson found a suitable audience for his poems in the family kitchen whenever he went home to Berneray.

In fact Dòmhnall made one poem which is a superb example of the old *bàrdachd baile* genre – 'Òran Step' (p. 58). Internal evidence suggests that it was composed not in his own community but in Grimsay, North Uist. He made other poems in, or about, the Grimsay area: 'Do Mhàiri NicillEathain, Griomsaigh' (p. 26), 'Griomsaigh' (p. 115) and 'Maighdeann Bhòidheach Chàirinis' ('The Lovely Girl from Carinish', p. 115). Further echoes of *bàrdachd baile* appear elsewhere, notably in 'An t-Seann Chaora' ('The Old Ewe', p. 85) and 'Na Solais Ùra' (p. 98). The latter is one of four poems on the coming of 'new lights' to South Lochboisdale (or to *Gleann na Ceòlraidh*, 'the Valley of Music', as he liked to call the district in his verse), the others being 'Angela' (p. 86), 'Fàilte Angela' (p. 115) and 'Fàilte Moira' (p. 115). Moira Macdonald and

Angela Binnie were newly-married girls who came to live in new houses in South Lochboisdale about 1990.

Of the 136 poems by Dòmhnall Aonghais Bhàin known to me at the time of writing, fifty or so are poems of nature, and another fifty or so are to women and girls. Only three are addressed to men: 'Am Bàrd' (p. 2), to the poet Donald John MacDonald (*Dòmhnall Iain Dhonnchaidh*, 1919–86); 'Fàilt' an t-Sagairt Òig' (p. 28), to Fr John Paul MacKinnon, who was ordained in St Peter's, Daliburgh, on 24 June 1999; and 'Marbhrann do Choinneach Mac a' Choisiche á Dalabrog' ('Elegy for Kenneth Walker from Daliburgh', p. 115). Walker died suddenly at the age of 27 in December 1985; his Gaelic surname should strictly be *Mac an Fhùcadair*, 'the Son of the Waulker', not *Mac a' Choisiche*, 'the Son of the Walker'. One nature poem, 'Cuairt Dhòmhnaill Iain feadh nan Gleann' ('Donald John's Walk around the Glens', p. 110) describes a sentimental tour around the South End by one of Dòmhnall's elder brothers. Donald John (a sailor) was a singer and a maker of songs, but this item is very much in our poet's own style.

Another dozen poems or so may be characterised as 'thoughts on death and change'. These include 'Cha Mhór Tha ri Àireamh' (p. 8), 'Caochladh' (p. 10), 'Cha Till an Òige (p. 14), 'Còmhradh an Eilthirich ris an Stuaidh' (p. 18), 'Triall na h-Ùine' (p. 64), 'Sgeulachdan nan Taighean-Céilidh' (p. 68), 'Seann Taigh-Solais Chalbhaigh' (p. 74), 'Ar Crìoch' ('Our End', p. 87), 'Fuaim an t-Sàile' ('The Sound of the Sea', p. 92), 'Gleann na Ceòlraidh 'nam Òige 's 'nam Aois' ('The Valley of Music in my Youth and Old Age', p. 115) and 'Sìth' ('Peace', p. 115).

'Triall na h-Ùine' is an absorbing set of reflections on the effect of ageing on the mind. In one's prime one should be confident, wise, self-assertive; instead one may become anxious and confused, even though, as the poet says, "Our course has come around / Those headlands that bedevilled us / And held us back upon our voyage." 'Seann Taigh-Solais Chalbhaigh' is in many ways Dòmhnall's most accessible piece, and it will certainly be a lasting one – the device of a talking lighthouse is appealing. 'Sgeulachdan nan Taighean-Céilidh' belongs to a minor genre in twentieth-century Gaelic verse, the ceilidh-house poem, of which I have given two examples elsewhere (*An Tuil* pp. 152, 404).

Another dozen poems or so can best be characterised as miscellaneous: one on a doll, one on Gaelic, one on a space-rocket, and so on. Two have to do with Eriskay, whose by-name is *Eilean na h-Òige* ('the Isle of Youth'), just as that of South Uist is *Eilean nan Crà-Ghèadh* ('the Isle of the Shelduck') or *Tìr an Eòrna* ('the Land of the Barley'). 'Eich Éirisgeigh' (p. 32) was commissioned by Comann Each nan Eilean (The Eriskay Pony Society) for their first stud book, soon to be published. When, late in life, Dòmhnall went once again over the hill to Kilbride ('Air Chuairt an Cille Bhrìghde', p. 114) or across the sound to Eriskay

('Cuairt a dh'Eilean na h-Òige', p. 96), the resulting poems carry something of the tone of a state visit.

Too much categorisation can of course be unhelpful. In the very fine 'Cumha' (p. 22) praise of girlhood merges seamlessly into reflections on death and change. The sentiment of 'An t-Eun Fuadain' (p. 8), which is a nature poem, is really not very far removed from that 'A' Mhaighdeann Chriadhadh' ('The Doll', *An Tuil* p. 512), which is not. I asked Dòmhnall whether the doll was flotsam picked up on the shore. "No," he replied. "The Doll was the toy of a young girl that was sitting beside me in church when the holiday people were at home. The girl's mother gave me a strange look when she saw me giving the doll the hand-shake of peace during Mass."

Like Duncan Ban Macintyre when describing the deer and their habitat on Ben Dorain, Dòmhnall is best as a nature poet when he gets into the detail. He names flowers, as at p. 38 and elsewhere. He makes poems to specific creatures such as 'An Iolaire' ('The Eagle', p. 114) or 'Don Uiseig' ('To the Lark', p. 114). I felt a little ashamed of having criticised the ubiquity of this theme, as I did at p. xl of *An Tuil*, when I read his words "I love the music of birds" (p. 9).

There are of course other variations on the 'nature' theme. In 'A' Bheinn' (p. 114) the mountain speaks to the poet, just as it did in William Ross's 'Còmhradh eadar am Bàrd agus Blà-bheinn' ('Conversation between the Poet and Blaven'). The emphasis is often on meteorology, nowhere more so than in 'Am Faoilteach 1984' ('January 1984', p. 82). 'Chan Eil Sinn gun Sùgradh' ('We Don't Lack Entertainment', p. 89) begins on an argumentative note. Sometimes nature offers a 'Hallaig'-type evocation of those who are gone, as in 'Bàgh Hartabhagh' (p. 16), 'A' Ghaoth an-Iar tha Séideadh thar na Mara' ('West Wind that Blows across the Sea', p. 80), and 'Siubhal Chluaintean' ('Walking the Meadows', p. 106).

Some of these are clearance poems as good as we have, given that the best clearance poems were not written till the twentieth century anyway (cf. *An Tuil* p. xlii). In 'Siubhal Chluaintean' the mood is one of happiness: "There are many contentments amongst these meadows," says Dòmhnall, because, as he goes on to point out, in the midst of the beauty of nature "although there's no buildings or people living there / love and kinship reigned once in the valleys of mist," and he goes on to describe the vanished community mainly in terms of sound: "the sound of the carding" (*fuaim a' chàrd'*), "the labour of quern grinding barley grain" (*saothair bhrà bleith nan grànlach eòrna*), "spinning-wheel busily humming" (*cuidheall-shnìomha gu dian ri crònan*), "violent blows being given to a shuttle there" (*buillean làidir gan toirt air spàl ann*), "dexterous women waulking the tweeds" (*mnathan làmhchair a' luadh nan clòithean*), while "joy and love on their friendly faces" are contrasted with the surrounding "peace of silence in the upland moors".

Sometimes nature slides into patriotism. It may be a patriotism (if that is the right word) for Dòmhnall's immediate *dùthchas* – 'Easaval-patriotism'. There is Uist-patriotism, represented over and over by the island's age-old symbols of *crà-ghèadh* ('shelduck') and *eòrna* ('barley'). There is Clan-Donald-patriotism, represented of course by *fraoch* ('heather'). There is no discernible Scottish patriotism, unless we may read this into the poet's frequent singling out of the *cluaran* ('thistle'). He does not call heather *fraoch* at all in the first stanza of 'Ri Iomall na Fairge' (p. 115), just *suaithneas Chlann Dòmhnaill*, "the badge of Clan Donald".

Uist is described at p. 37 as "the land that nurtured the thistle (*cluaran*) that will always be our symbol". At p. 66 the island is proudly said to nurture *slàn-lusan is cluarain . . . / nach mill gaoth tuath no reòdh* ("healing plants and thistles / which no north wind or frost can destroy"), and as the *cluaran* is not itself a healing plant, its status as the symbol of Scottish nationhood must be what Dòmhnall had in mind. Again, at p. 84 he points out to Easaval with no hint of irony that *bidh cluaran uaine frìth-bhacach 'na dhìleab dhut gu bràch* ("a pale-green barbed thistle will be your inheritance for ever"). Finally, at p. 106 he declares that "the spear-thistle (*cluaran-deilgneach*) is a precious symbol / while the lovely primrose by the burn's so glorious." Above all other members of its tribe it is the prickly spear-thistle which represents Scotland.

On one occasion, and one only, a view of nature slides into a view of politics. This is in 'Taigh Sgoile Glaic Ruairidh' (p. 113), where Dòmhnall recalls his education in the little school which stood by itself in upper Glendale. "Our clothes weren't pricey, / We knew nothing of silk, / No treasures of elegance covered us — / Our only inheritance / Was the hardship of inferiority / Which kept us down in the ditch to our noses."

Man is very much part of nature, as where he appears duly in the annual cycle in just one verse of the nature-oriented 'An t-Eilean Àghmhor Bòidheach' ('The Prosperous Lovely Island', p. 114):

Bidh Oidhch' Shamhna, mar bha i riamh,
    Gar riarachadh le sòlas
Nuair bhios an òigridh oirnn mun cuairt
    A' gabhail duain is òrain.

("Hallowe'en, as it has alway done, / Will entertain us mightily / When the young folk come to call on us / Performing songs and rhymes.") Fair enough, since this is the point of the year in which life moves indoors. In a poem like 'Mo Dhùrachd Thu Thilleadh' ('I Wish You'd Return', p. 101) nature and woman are counterpoised:

The shining of the sun
In the young maytime morning
Is the picture I'll make of you,
        Gold-jewel of the white palms.

The fourth verse of 'Angela' (p. 86) offers another concise example of this technique, while it is applied more extensively in 'An Rìbhinn Bhòidheach' (p. 114). 'Tìr nan Raon' (p. 40) moves from being a standard nature poem to being perhaps Dòmhnall Aonghais Bhàin's outstanding poem of material culture, more so even than 'Taigh-Tasgaidh Chill Donnain' (p. 72). Thus in different ways are man and nature placed in exquisite balance.

How Dòmhnall approached his nature poems is clear: he walked the territory with his ears and eyes open and knew it intimately. How, then, did he approach his poems to women? Sometimes the vision seems abstract or distantly remembered. 'Bean na Buana' ('The Harvest Woman', p. 114) owes not a little to Wordsworth's 'Highland Lass'. Elsewhere one is struck by Dòmhnall's shyness, as when he tells us that the woman or girl whom he is praising is one that he has spotted at Mass (see 'Maighdeann Loch a' Mhuilinn', *Voice of the Bard* p. 23). Then there are poems inspired by pictures. In 'Dealbh Camilla' (p. 24) the picture is in a newspaper, while 'Dealbh Essie Stiùbhairt' (p. 114) begins

An leabhar-eachdraidh an luchd-cuairte
Dhearc mo shùil air dealbh na gruagaich;
Thug a h-ìomhaigh aoibheil shuairce
Iomadh bruadar gu mo smaoin.

("In the visitors' record-book / I noticed the girl's picture; / Her lovely kindly appearance / Brought many dreams to my thoughts.") There were also the nurses and other women who helped him and tended him in his various illnesses, to many of whom he sent poems of thanks. A note on his manuscript of 'Don Té Rinn Tighinn gam Fheòraich Dhachaigh' (p. 30, on the head of the home help service) says: "Drawing water to my own mill." By contrast, in 'Cumha' (p. 23) he says, "I can picture your handsome features in the grave / Although I never saw you in the flesh." Finally, in 'Ina' (p. 111) he seems to have got a bit carried away. "I'm in the seventh heaven — / The King of Glory pitied me / When I got a Fair Maid / Who'll keep me warm from the cold. / In the morning she makes tea / And rakes for me the ashes, / She cleans out my stove-pipe — / All done before I stir. / She puts a meal on the table, / Soup and meat as is proper; / At the weekend we have fish, / And a bottle of wine on occasion. / All is as I'd want it, / The wheel of fortune has turned — / A pension and a scratch card / And a blonde on the pillow. / A thousand curses on my folly, / Much damage results from it; / From all the seed sown in my youth / I could be reaping oats and barley."

'Mo Reul Iùil' (p. 54) is I believe one of the outstanding Gaelic love poems of the twentieth century, fit to rank with James MacLeod's 'A' Cheist' and Sorley MacLean's 'A' Bhuaile Ghréine' (*An Tuil* pp. 88, 292). Dòmhnall appears to have told Timothy Neat: "I enjoy the company of women, but I'm not a man was ever wildly in love, not like Byron, not like the poets you read about. I have written poems for women but it's not love poetry that I write." (*Voice of the Bard* p. 20.) Nevertheless there is an autobiographic passion in 'Mo Reul Iùil' which the poem's title serves to underline. "Those terrifying clouds have gone / And love's come in their place, / Hospitality's sun has risen / And the gentleness of May . . ." His verse about the woman's hair is a *tour de force* of its kind, reminiscent of William Ross's

S bachlach dualach cas-bhuidh cuachach
Càradh suaineis gruag do chinn,
Gu h-àlainn bòidheach fàinneach òr-bhuidh
An caraibh seòighn 's an òrdugh grinn.

("Curly, wavy, yellow-wreathed, cupped / Is the twisting form of the hair of your head, / Beautiful, gorgeous, ringletted, yellow-gold, / In amazing curves and perfect arrangement.") Eighteenth-century verse had equipped the Gaelic language with an astonishing range of vocabulary for the hair, and Dòmhnall deploys it masterfully. But it is more than mere vocabulary, and ultimately outdoes Ross, for when Dòmhnall declares triumphantly that "it's lovely round your shoulders, / lending elegance and charm", one thinks of the power deployed by an attractive woman over a man's mind when she unties her hair and it springs out to be cast free over her neck with a flick of the wrist. But as with Mór Ros, the older woman with whom William Ross was infatuated, there are clear indications in 'Mo Reul Iùil' that the poet's relationship with his subject was not a physical one. Close focus alternates with a more distant one, and seems like a focus of eye, as in a crowded room, rather than of touch. She may be the same *reul iùil* as is addressed in 'Ged Shéideadh a' Ghailleann san Fhaoilteach' ('Though the Storm in the Wolftime may Blow', p. 115):

Reul iùil thu an doimhne na h-iarmailt
A' deàrrsadh nas briagha na càch.

("You're a guiding star in the infinity of space / Shining more beautifully than the rest.")

If 'Mo Reul Iùil' is the finest of Dòmhnall's poems to women, 'Mìosan na Bliadhna' is surely the finest of his poems to nature. It is relatively epic in scope – 158 lines long, it characterises each month of the year in turn with sharply-turned lyricism – but, unlike 'Mo Reul Iùil', it is also experimental in conception. It begins regularly (but excitingly) in January with three quatrains, each of which consists of three lines of four stresses, linked with end-rhyme, and a short fourth line of two stresses, the three short lines linked to each other by end-rhyme. February follows the same pattern except that the short lines are not fully linked by end-rhyme. In March the break-up of the pattern continues: the long lines are arranged in sets of three, two, three and one respectively, and both elements of the rhyming system are disrupted.

The same can be said for April, except that the long lines are arranged this time in sets of three, three, two and one. May extends the anarchy further by introducing a block of four long lines consisting of two rhyming couplets. June is the same, but longer. July is longer still, but while the sets of long lines rhyme correctly, the short ones do not. In August there is only one short line (the third), the rest consisting entirely of long lines in rhyming couplets. September puts that into reverse, consisting of four rhyming couplets (that is, if we may allow *saoibhir : ghamhnan* as a rhyme) and a 'perfect' quatrain of the kind not found since July. October consists of five perfect rhyming couplets. November is broadly similar to August but has an extra long line which rhymes with nothing whatever. Finally December consists of six rhyming couplets except that the rhyme in the first is imperfect – *docair : dòbhaidh.*

Dòmhnall Aonghais Bhàin was steeped in traditional metres while becoming increasingly surrounded by the new 'free' verse of the twentieth century, and he had clearly decided to carve out a little piece of freedom of his own. Rhythmic discipline is maintained in 'Mìosan na Bliadhna' by the fact that all lines are of four stresses or two, and there is a good deal of consistency in rhyme and in the shape and length of verses, but what he is rejecting here is the automatic precedence of form over meaning. In 1987 I wrote: "Traditional poetry was thirled to rhyme and generally sung; its patterns were mesmeric, and at its worst it followed clichés like railway tracks." (*The History of Scottish Literature, Volume 4: Twentieth Century*, ed. by Cairns Craig for Aberdeen University Press, p. 205.) Dòmhnall had begun to publish 'Mìosan na Bliadhna' four years earlier (in *Am Pàipear*), but nevertheless my comment represents the sort of criticism to which the poem appears to be a response.

While it cannot be argued that Dòmhnall had a great talent for the unexpected – the last couplets of 'Bagh Hartabhagh' (p. 18) and 'Loch Cheàrsanais' (p. 95) being possible exceptions – the precedence of meaning over form reappears here and there, nicely confirming his own definition of his work as *réimis gun daors'* ("unslavish rhyming", p. 89). In the thoughtful couplet

Tha eachdraidh anns na taighean fàs
'S beachd-smaointeachadh ri fheòrach

(p. 12) the demands of *aicill* ('internal rhyme') are ignored. In 'An Rocaid' (p. 4) he produced a very acceptable piece of free verse on a distinctly twentieth-century topic, while in 'Mo Mhac-Meanma 's mo Pheann air Chuairt' ('My Imagination and Pen Go for a Walk', p. 115) he experiments with semantics.

Théid sinn cuairt air chéilidh am measg charraig gheura chàrn
Far an tionail sinn clàr-mìneachaidh tro fhoghlam sìth na tlàiths.

("We will go around ceilidhing amongst the sharp rocks of stonepiles / Where we'll gather a glossary by studying the peace of tranquillity.") The point he is making by mixing the metaphors of nature and of learning is, of course, the educative value of the environment. The theme is also found in 'Siubhal Chluaintean' (p. 107):

'S ged dhìobair foghlam dhiubh tiodhlaic chungaidh
Bu deàrrsant' cliùmhor bha iùil an eòlais.

("And although education has banished from them the gifts of medicine / Brilliant and celebrated was their scientific knowledge.")

Dòmhnall's ability as a lyric poet, mentioned above, may also be seen in 'Cha Till an Òige' (p. 14), 'Cumha' (p. 22), 'Chì Mi Bhuam' ('I See Afar', p. 87) and 'Ròs na Mórchuis' ('The Rose of Splendour', p. 101). In 'Chì Mi Bhuam', in an almost shamanic condition at the end of a litany of nature he arrives – involuntarily, so to speak – at woman-as-nature: "I see the golden-haired girl — / I often think of her beauty / For she's lovely as the rose / Under fresh morning dew." He does this again in 'Eilean Àghmhor nam Buadh' (p. 114):

Ann an Uibhist an eòrn' tha rìbhinnean òg'
A tha loinneil 'nan dòigh 's 'nam beusan,
An gruaidhean mar ròs am measg cluaintean an fheòir
Anns an ùr-mhadainn bhòidhich chéitein.

("Uist of the barley can boast of young girls / Who are fine in their ways and behaviour, / Their cheeks like a rose amidst meadows of grass / In the lovely fresh morning of maytime.") It is curiously reminiscent of the habit of the learned classical Gaelic poets – including the MacMhuirichs who served the Clanranalds in Uist down to within 200 years of Dòmhnall's lifetime – of rounding off a poem to a chief with a verse or two of less formal praise to the man's wife or daughter. Such 'women's verses' often contain more genuine feeling than all the rest of the poem put together.

In 'Mo Reul Iùil' the reverse happens – in its final verse, following the unfollowable "And if I could get what I'd ask for, / You'll have the gift of life eternal", Dòmhnall Aonghais Bhàin's greatest lovesong reverts to nature. "In blue-green Uist of the barley / You grew up when you were young / Where the ever-murmuring waves / Debate upon the beach — / Where the heather of Clan Donald / Covers the high hills / And where the dove will make its home / As it likes to, in the rocks." There is both lyricism and symbolism here, but not lyricism or symbolism which would be seen by the non-Gaelic-speaker as having anything to do with love.

First, the woman is located in her *dùthchas*, using symbols of fertility: *gorm*, the colour of rich healthy growth; *eòrna*, 'barley'. Second, the *dùthchas* is made real by an appeal to sound. Third, kinship: her blood must be good. Fourth, in Dòmhnall's almost filmic conclusion, the dove is the symbol of peace, but more than that, of love – it is hard not to be reminded of the ending of the well-known traditional song 'Bothan Àirigh am Bràigh Raithneach' ('A Shieling Bothy in Brae Rannoch') in which the girl fantasises about sleeping with her lover in the depths of the moor:

Bhiodh a' chuthag 's an smùdan
 A' gabhail ciùil dhuinn air chrannaibh.

Bhiodh an damh donn sa bhùireadh
 Gar dùsgadh sa mhadainn.

("The cuckoo and the ring-dove / Would sing us music on branches. / The brown stag with his bellowing / Would wake us up in the morning.")

'Mar a dh'Fhiosraich Mi Thu' ('As I Got to Know You', p. 99) is far from being an ordinary lovesong. It is quite strange and certainly lyrical, and employs a sophisticated symbolism. In the first verse there is a direct relationship between the woman and poetic inspiration: the symbolism is operating on two levels.

Se 'n gàire 'nad shùil teudan mo chiùil an àird.

("The smile in your eye is the strings of my music uplifted.") In the second verse a mediating symbol is introduced: having been stimulated, poetic inspiration becomes a vessel, whose destination is the fulfilment of desire. Whether that desire is the fulfilment of passion or the attainment of artistic goals is uncertain, but then, for poets, such ambiguity is normal. "My thought's imagination with melody light and smooth / Has sent my ship through the kyle with white sails and a following wind; / Dead water being under her prow, inactive, level and mild / Will bear me with joy to the haven of my own desire." In the third verse the maritime symbolism is retained but while the wind is present, the ship is re-interpreted first as *mo sgeul* ("my tale") and then, intriguingly, as

Lìonmhorachd ròs agus liosan nas bòidhche na ubhal.

("A fullness of roses and gardens lovelier than an apple.") This, then, is the gift, or the good wishes, which the poet is sending to his loved one, and as he reaches his climax in the penultimate verse the paradisaic theme is lyrically developed. Happiness is defined in familiar terms in the first three lines, but in the fourth the poet concedes, as it were, that the flora and fauna of Easaval may not be everyone's idea of perfect bliss, and tries with an effort to slip his imagination into a lady's shoe: "May each happiness swim like a swan on the top of the billows, / Each gracenote and chorus like the birds of the skies without gloom, / Like the riverside primrose that spring brings across on a visit — / Or like the maiden of Troy who launched a fleet to the ocean." The nautical love-messenger symbol can now be tidied away, for the poet's imagination has at last brought him into the 'physical' presence of the object of his thoughts. "The anchor's caught fast on the sea-bed and will not move, / There's no need for the sails, they are folded tightly and hard; / Each affair has its end, the wheel merrily goes around / And I see as I wanted — like before — the flush in your cheek."

Donald's English was not good, and he knew it. In 'A' Ghàidhlig' (p. 80) he says: "Though my English is weak, without much substance or subtlety, / It's absence won't condemn me in my visit to this life." He wrote at least five of his poems in English, however (see pp. 114–15), and attempted English translations of a number of others. A few of these have been used in this book, with some minimal editing by Jacqueline and Henry Marsh (Dòmhnall used 'tranquil' as a noun, for example). These have been marked 'author's translation'. Otherwise the translations in this book are my own, and are intended to reflect the rhythm of the original; in addition, a hint of rhyming structures is provided by indentation. The poems are arranged in no particular order.

I would like to thank all those who have contributed to this project: Jacqueline Marsh and Henry Marsh (Edinburgh); Mrs Christina Campbell (Dòmhnall's sister) and Katie Mary Campbell (his neighbour); Angus Peter Campbell; Alick and Roderick O'Henley; the Gaelic Books Council staff in Glasgow; Eòghann MacLachlainn; Helen Forbes; Liz Short; and, last but not least, my wife Máire for typesetting and maps. I am also grateful to the editors of *The Stornoway Gazette*, *Am Pàipear*, *Gairm*, *The Scotsman* and *The Voice of the Bard* for permission to reproduce poems which appeared in their publications.

I think Dòmhnall would have been surprised to know just how soon after his death there would be a book of his poems, and I hope he would have liked it. *A chuid de phàrras dha.* He lies at peace exactly where he wanted to be, with his friends in Cnoc Hàllainn, but poetically speaking his spirit will always be somewhere on Easaval. Especially on a day like today.

Peebles, 21 June 2000

Am Bàrd

Ailig O Hianlaidh

Bha mi san éisteachd an latha a chaidh bàs Dhòmhnaill Aonghais Bhàin eubhach ann an eaglais Ghearraidh na Mònadh. Sa mhionaid a thàinig an naidheachd á beul an t-sagairt sgaoil osna thùrsach aonaghuthach á measg na bha làthair. Chan ann tric a chuala mi a leithid a' tachairt riamh ach bha e 'na chomharra air a' mheas a bh' aig muinntir Uibhist a-Deas air Dòmhnall, an dà chuid mar dhuine agus mar bhàrd.

Cha robh mi fhéin ach gu math òg an uair a chuir mi eòlas air Dòmhnall an toiseach. Bha e ag obair còmhla ri m' athair aig an t-seann fhactaraidh feamainn am Baghasdal agus tha cuimhn' agam aon fheasgar a bhith muigh a' siubhal chaorach air Beinn Éiseabhail an uair a thadhail sinn air an taigh aige. Fada mus tigeadh an taigh tughaidh beag grinn am follais, chitheadh tu an toit bhon t-simileir ag éirigh os cionn nan cnoc, agus a' coimhead air ais an-diugh chan urrainn dhomh gun a bhith smaointinn ach gun robh an toit sin mar shamhla air bàrdachd Dhòmhnaill fhéin – a' cumail fios ris an t-saoghal mhór a-muigh mu shaoghal eile a tha cha mhór air a dhol á sealladh agus mun eilean agus na daoine air an robh uiread de ghràdh aige fhéin.

Cha robh taigh tughaidh 'na annas sam bith dhòmhsa aig an àm oir chuir mi seachad a' chiad sia bliadhna dhe m' bheatha fhéin a' fuireach ann am fear dhiubh agus chun an latha an-diugh tha mi cumail a-mach nach robh mi riamh ann an taighean a bha cho cofhartail riutha. Cha robh taigh Dhòmhnaill air a chaochladh – seann teine *Modern Mistress* le braidseal math mònadh, an coire a' goil 'na mhullach agus beingidh ris an uinneig an-ear far am faigheadh tu éisteachd ris na faclan socair siùbhlach a thigeadh bho Dhòmhnall fhéin aig ceann an teine. Mhothaich mi a' chiad thrup sin gun robh an t-uabhas de chanastairean tì aige os cionn an teine agus an uair a dh'fhaighnichear dha car son a bha na h-uidhir dhiubh ann thuirt e nach b' urrainn dha bhith uair sam bith ás aonais na tì! S neònach mur e tiodhlagan a bh' unnta bho chàirdean a bhiodh a' tadhal air agus is neònach cuideachd mura robh an eachdraidh inntinneach fhéin aig gach fear dhiubh.

Ach gheibheadh tu barrachd is tì aig Dòmhnall bochd agus riamh bhon uair sin bhiodh e faighneachd ciamar a bha dol dhomh agus ag iarraidh orm a' Ghàidhlig a chumail suas, aig àm an uair a bha cuid a thidsearan gam chomhairleachadh cùl a chur rithe. Chithinn e aig an eaglais Di-Dòmhnaich agus bhiodh an còmhnaidh ceistean aige a thaobh na bàird a bha mi leughadh, gu sònraichte as déidh dhomh dhol dhan Oilthigh. Cha d'fhuair e fhéin, coltach ri móran dhe ghinealach, cothrom air foghlam àrd ìre ann, ach 'na dhòigh fhéin bha e cheart cho fiosrach mu na bàird mhóra leithid Wordsworth is Byron 's a bha duine ris an do choinnich mi riamh ann an oilthigh.

Bha meas mór aige cuideachd air an obair aig Donnchadh Bàn Mac an t-Saoir, gu sònraichte na dàin a bha déiligeadh ri nàdar. Sin far an robh an ùidh aig Dòmhnall fhéin, a' cur an céill bòidhchead na sgìre agus a' dèanamh luaidh air na daoine a bha mun cuairt air. Mar sin dhòmhsa co-dhiù chan e bàrd baile a bh' ann an Dòmhnall idir mar a chanas cuid ach bàrd nàdair. Chithear sin sa mhórchuid dhen obair aige ach gu sònraichte ann an dàin leithid 'Eilean Uibhist' agus 'Mìosan na Bliadhna' far a bheil an dàimh eadar am bàrd agus a chuspair fuaighte ri chéile cho làidir 's a ghabhas.

Chan eil sin ag ràdh nach robh taobhannan eile air Dòmhnall ge-tà. An-dràst 's a-rithist chuireadh e iongnadh ort an uair a nochdadh dàn leithid 'An Rocaid', a chaidh a sgrìobhadh air son clann, neo 'Dealbh Camilla', a chòrd cho mór ri Prionnsa na Cuimrigh 's gun do chuir e litir gu Dòmhnall ga mholadh air son a chuid saothair! Ach sann san dùthaich mu chuairt air an robh an ùidh as motha aige agus tha fiosam gur e sin na dàin a thug an toileachadh as motha dha.

As déidh ceumnachadh chuir mi seachad grunnd fheasgraichean còmhla ri Dòmhnall 's mi lorg fhaclan air son faclair ùr Gàidhlig a bha Oilthigh Ghlaschu a' dèanamh. Aig an àm tha cuimhn' agam a bhith ag innse dha gun robh mi fhéin air a bhith riasladh le bloighean rannan a chur ri chéile agus ged nach robh iad faisg cho coileanta neo cho briathrach ris an obair aige fhéin, cha dhìochuimhnich mi gu bràth na faclan còir agus an deagh chomhairle a thug e orm – "Cum ort a' sgrìobhadh agus na biodh leisg sam bith ort do chuid obair a chur an clò."

Nise do dhaoine a bha eòlach air Dòmhnall s dòcha gu bheil e doirbh a chreidsinn gun canadh e leithid oir a dh'ainneoin 's gun robh e sgrìobhadh a' mhórchuid dhe bheatha, cha robh dad a mhiann aige a chuid obrach fhoillseachadh agus gu dearbh tha e coltach gun do loisg e gu leòr dhe na dàin a rinn e an toiseach agus is mór am beud sin cuideachd. Coltach ri móran eile a dh'fheuch ri bàrdachd a sgrìobhadh cha robh e smaointinn gun robh dad a dh'fheum anns na bha e dèanamh agus ann an dòigh bha an suidheachadh aigesan nas duilghe buileach a chionns gun deach a thogail ann an àite a bha taomadh le daoine a bha 'nan sàr bhàird.

S cinnteach nach eil baile eile an Uibhist neo an eilean sam bith coltach ri Taobh a-Deas Loch Baghasdail a thaobh na thàinig ás de bhàird, agus b'e 'n rud a b' annasaiche buileach gur ann dhan aon teaghlach a bhuineadh iad. Bha Seonaidh mac Dhòmhnaill 'ic Iain Bhàin agus a bhràthair Iain ann agus gu h-iongantach bha ceathrar dhe na mic aig Iain 'nam bàird cuideachd – Seumas, an duine aig Curstaidh, piuthar Dhòmhnaill; a bhràithrean Aonghas Iain agus Iain, am fear a rinn an t-òran 'Soraidh Leat a Dhòmhnaill Ruairidh' an uair a bha e falbh a-null a New Zealand; agus os an cionn sin uile bha Ruairidh, neo an 'Ròidseag' mar a b' fheàrr a dh'aithnichear e, am fear a rinn an t-òran ainmeil 'A Pheigi a Ghràidh'.

Chan iarradh bàrd òg a chiùird ionnsachadh bho dhaoine na b' fheàrr na iad sin, ach bha an t-slat tomhais a chuir iad romhpa duilich a toirt a-mach cuideachd. Bha deagh fhios aig Dòmhnall air a-sin agus bha e coimhead suas gu mór ris an 'Ròidseag' gu sònraichte. Ach mu dheireadh fhuair e seachad air na duilgheadasan sin, agus tha sinn uile toilichte gun d'fhuair.

Gu h-annasach an uair a bha mi aig an taigh bho chionn ghoirid chaidh mi seachad air taigh Dhòmhnaill agus bha clann a pheathar ga fhalamhachadh. Bhuail e orm gur mór am beud mura téid an taigh sin a ghléidheadh 's a thionndadh 'na àite far an gabhadh cuimhne a chumail, chan ann a-mhàin air obair Dhòmhnaill ach cuideachd air na bàird eile a dh'ainmich mi 's a thàinig á Taobh a-Deas Loch Baghasdail agus nach d'fhuair riamh a' chliù air an robh iad airidh. Chan eil mi cinnteach co-dhiùbh a bhiodh sin ciallach neo cuibheasach, ach se tàmailt a bhiodh ann mura biodh an taigh beag grinn ud fhathast ri fhaicinn sna bliadhnaichean a tha romhainn.

Ach s math an rud gu bheil na dàin aig Dòmhnall a-nis ri'm faighinn san leabhar sa agus tha mi moiteil ga-rìreabh gun deach iarraidh orm mo smuaintean fhéin mu Dhòmhnall a chur 'na thoiseach. Bidh cuimhn' agamsa air Dòmhnall mar fhear a chuir bòidhchead Ceann a-Deas Uibhist an céill le briathran snasail snog, ach os cionn sin bidh cuimhn 'am air mar dhuine gun smal a dh'fheuchadh ris an rud a b' fheàrr fhaicinn sa h-uile duine. Fiùs an uair a bha e smaointinn air deireadh a làithean b'e an t-eilean 's na daoine bu mhotha a bh' air aire, agus bhiodh e iomchaidh seo a thoirt gu ceann leis na faclan aige fhéin san rann mu dheireadh de 'Eilean Uibhist'.

Nuair thig an cadal buan 's nach cuir mi feum air cluasaig
    'S a chàirear leis an t-sluagh mi san fhuar-leabaidh dhùint',
A' ghainmheach bhith mun cuairt dhomh 's am muran gorm mu m' uachdar
    'S an duslach anns 'n do ghluais mi gam chuartach' as ùr,
Mhiannaichinn bhith 'n càradh measg eòlach agus chàirdean
    ('S gur pailt iad ann a Hàllann a' cnàmh anns an ùir)
Ann an eilean gorm mo shinnsear, mu'n d'rinn mi seo a sgrìobhadh
    A théid a sheinn gu cinnteach le binn-bheul a' chiùil.

The Poet

Henry Marsh

Donald Macdonald of South Lochboisdale died in hospital in Glasgow on 5th March, 2000. The youngest of a family of four, he was born on 12th December 1926, and raised on the family croft. It is a spot of great beauty but it is now difficult to imagine how health and happiness could be sustained on four acres of such moorland with its characteristic admixture of rock and bog. There was enough to sustain two cows and an adequate supply of potatoes. The sheep had access to common grazing and peat for fuel was plentiful. It is interesting that Donald often talked about the hardness of such a life – with its monotonous winter diet of salt herring and potatoes – but, in common with many of his island contemporaries, he had no sense of poverty. This suggests that whatever the circumstances their lives were associated with fulfilment. Indeed, he referred to crofting as 'a beautiful life'.

Getting to school involved a walk of two miles over the moor to what he affectionately described as the 'tin hut' at Glendale. The children went barefoot in summer. They ate their pieces as soon as they arrived and, except for some milk at lunchtime, went hungry for the rest of the day. Margaret Fay Shaw, the American who collected songs and made a remarkable record of life in South Uist in photograph and film, was gratefully remembered as having made soup for the children at lunchtime. Donald recalled his schooldays with great affection and considered that he had been well taught. It is remarkable that many islanders of his generation are not literate in Gaelic because they were taught to write only in English.

Theirs was a home where Donald's imagination was shaped by the songs, stories, music and talk that he recalls in his poem 'The Tales of the Ceilidh-Houses' (p. 69). Unusually for a bard amidst this tradition Donald, unlike his mother, was no singer and composed few songs. It may have been that his schooling, which was in English, brought to his sensibility something of the Romantic tradition. He talked warmly of his young teacher, Annie Macphee, introducing him to Wordsworth, Shelley, Keats and, particularly, to Byron.

It was to nature, then, that he looked for his inspiration and to the beauty of women – he carefully distinguished such celebratory 'praise poems' from love poetry. Yet 'nature' is hardly an adequate concept. Though no self-conscious explorer of language, Donald resembled Gerard Manley Hopkins in this – much of what he wrote was in celebration of the Creation.

Perhaps it was the influence of both the Gaelic and English traditions that made Donald's work so distinctive. Yet the price of this departure from orthodoxy, in a naturally shy man, may have been his great reticence regarding his poetry. For much of his life he composed in secret and, indeed, he destroyed his early work. His sister, Chrissy Campbell, had married into a family of bards and singers and perhaps this too generated its own pressures. It was Mary Maclean, the bardess from Grimsay (see p. 27), who recognised the quality of his work and encouraged him to have his poems published. They appeared in the *Stornoway Gazette*, in *Am Pàipear*, published in Benbecula, *The Scotsman* and in the Gaelic literary magazine, *Gairm*. In 1983 he won first prize for Gaelic Bardachd at the National Mod, the annual Gaelic festival of music and literature.

Towards the end of his life Donald began to achieve wider recognition. He did a number of radio broadcasts and appeared in television programmes including 'Myth and Magic' and Bill Bryson's 'Notes from a Small Island'. The invitation to open the new museum at Kildonan gave him very great pleasure (see 'Taigh Tasgaidh Chill Donnain', p. 72). For once he was 'the big shot'. He posted wee pieces of the ribbon to his friends. Perhaps most significantly, he featured as one of fourteen bards in Timothy Neat's beautiful and evocative book, *The Voice of the Bard*. A haunting photograph of Donald was used for the front cover. The profile could have come from a Renaissance medallion. The book was launched at the Edinburgh Book Festival in August 1999.

On that occasion, as he stood to recite some of his poems, he was a shy, rather frail figure. Then with his sonorous, beautifully cadenced Gaelic poetry he caught his audience. A few evenings later, in a BBC studio, he won all hearts and minds with his stories and reminiscences. The staff simply delighted in him.

Donald stayed for a week with us at that time. He had never been to the capital before. Worried that we would not recognise him at Waverley Station he gave us a careful account of how he would be dressed, down to the dark blue tie 'with the small design of a crown'. He would also wear his cap which 'very few people wear these days'. But the stamp of his face could never be missed, even at a busy station. He took great delight in the beauty of Edinburgh. At first, we were disconcerted by the modesty of his requirements. Every evening he ate 'boiled steak' and potatoes and, otherwise, had the occasional piece of toast. We now realise that this regimen was the only way he could cope with his illness.

Donald never knew his father, Angus Macdonald, who had died from a stomach ulcer, seven months after the child was born. Margaret Fay Shaw mentions in her book that many people on the island had stomach ulcers and suggests that one of the reasons was the salt ingested with the salt herring – the fish were washed rather than soaked before cooking. Though Donald was known as a strong man in his prime – Donald 'the crane' – he was plagued by ill health himself. He wrote in a letter, "My hospital life goes like this. Seven times in our own hospital, twice in Canniesburn, twice in the Western Infirmary, once in the Royal Infirmary, the County Hospital Invergordon, the Lewis Hospital and Raigmore." When an ulcer was removed in 1961 there followed what he described as the happiest days of his life. He was released both from the terrible pain and from drinking to relieve it, a habit which no doubt had contributed to his worsening condition and his accompanying depression. Poetry came from this release and, as always, it was associated with times of fulfilment and happiness.

As he recounted his stories it was often very difficult to establish when the events had taken place. When he first told us a tale of Clanranald of Ormaclate being haunted by a toad it was as if the events had occurred the previous week. This was fascinating testimony that Donald was, in important ways, the practitioner of a living tradition.

It seems that Clanranald had built a fine house for his aristocratic French bride who was not too delighted with her situation on the machair, surrounded by mountains to the east and an ocean to the west. Some items went missing in the house and a servant girl was seized and tied to the seaweed by her hair so that she would reveal the culprit. She never did and was drowned as the tide rose. Ever afterwards, everywhere he went, Clanranald was accompanied by a toad. Only on one occasion, when he was about to set sail for Skye, did he seem about to escape its company. The toad was nowhere to be seen. But contrary winds delayed the sailing. After a frustrating week the toad hopped on to the quay and boarded the ship. At that moment the wind changed and the ship could set sail.

Donald told his stories with a gentle but almost incantatory intensity – indeed the Clanranald story loses much of its effect when deprived of the exceptionally long vowel that he gave to the 'toad'.

Listening to the conversation and tales he exchanged with Mary Maclean, was it safe to assume that in the Uists bardesses were still regarded with great suspicion and buried face down to prevent them from uttering maledictions? Could people still find themselves magically transported twenty miles without the aid of car, helicopter or whisky? Could this explain why, despite the tramping of generations, there was no path to Donald's door?

If time collapsed for the listener in such circumstances so too did the concept of the nuclear family. Donald lived in a community and, in his distinctive way, helped to foster and sustain it. I remember him talking to a complete stranger, brought up in North Uist, and after two hours of meticulous genealogical research, a great network of mutual friends and family connections was unearthed and the health and well being of all concerned duly exchanged. Like his forebears, he was the keeper of a genealogical tradition and in that, and many other ways, he represented for us a world that has largely been lost, so that he was far more important for us than he could ever, in his modesty, have imagined. This is not a matter of nostalgia. In the passing of Donald and people like him we are losing touch with important ways of being in the world.

After leaving school at fourteen Donald did a number of odd jobs about the crofts. It was while he was engaged in the fishing out of Lochboisdale that he became involved in the events that were recorded in Sir Compton Mackenzie's *Whisky Galore.* The *SS Politician* came to grief in the Sound of Eriskay. Because of the oil associated with the wreck, salvaging the whisky was a difficult and dangerous business. The crates were spirited away and buried by the crofts. Gardening in the dark became unusually popular that summer. But there was, in the end, a price to pay. Because of the 'distraction' the harvest was poor – "It did nobody any good."

For a time he worked on the mainland on building sites, at a hydro-electric scheme and with the Forestry Commission. He returned to the islands to work with contractors in Lochboisdale and Benbecula. Later in life he gave up work to look after his mother while she was suffering from senile dementia. His sister and the neighbours were a great support. Until near the end his mother remained physically strong. She was often very active at night. On one occasion she took a stick to him while he was asleep thinking he was an intruder. He looked after her for five difficult years. In a fundamental way he was exhausted by the experience but, typically, he had no regrets.

The last year of his working life was spent on a job-creation scheme (see 'Òran Step', p. 58) but before that, for nine years, he worked at the alginates factory. The work was very heavy and boring but concentration was needed to keep the machines working. To get there involved a walk of four miles, which, many a time, because of shift work had to be undertaken on pitch dark winter nights in wind and rain. Donald was also aware that one of the dips in the road had the reputation of being haunted. He very much enjoyed excursions into the supernatural and this emerged in the television programme 'Music and Myth' where he talked about traditional stories involving fairies and water horses.

He was eventually to receive a small pension from the company. It was through this and the state pension that Donald in his latter years at last found financial security. It was a measure of the man that with this modest provision he considered himself entirely contented and better off than he had ever been in his life.

There was something compelling about Donald. It was not only that he had roots in the community and in his faith and in the bardic tradition – he was also, somehow, at one with the landscape. He had the authenticity of a tree or a rock. It was as if he had survived the hardships and suffering in his life somehow strengthened. The constant stream of visitors was, no doubt, attracted at first, by his reputation as a bard or his picturesque thatched cottage. But people returned again and again. He had an international correspondence. His kindness and natural courtesy were enriching – people left the better for having encountered him. This was felt by everyone who knew him – shop assistants, nurses, family and friends.

After he died my wife sat down to write that most difficult of letters, of condolence, to his sister Chrissy. I felt moved to contribute. After twenty years of silence I found myself writing a verse. A few days before we had been at the memorable first Scottish performance of Wagner's opera, 'Parsifal'. There was no magic to heal Donald, though, in a certain way, death can make a life more vivid.

For Donald Macdonald of South Lochboisdale

Parsifal sang as you lay dying.
But there was no wound-healing spear for you —
Only the surgeon's blade. You were caught
In a maze of streets and circumstance,
Far from the white strands where the curled
Atlantic surged in a north wind,
When the light in your handful of stardust failed.
Though I am blind to your language I knew
You through your land as I know myself
Through Grampian's heights where tumbling pipits
Sing over the grey rocks and the eagle
Soars. I remember from another world
The track to South Lochboisdale
And a jewelled mirror glittering in the sun:
'This is where I do my composing'.
Whatever you sang it was your serenity and the smiling
Gravity of your kindness that drew the heart.

Am Bàrd

Fàilt' ort fhéin, a charaid bhàird,
Siud dhuit mo làmh gam dheòin —
Bu tric a thog thu m' inntinn àrd
Le tàlantan do bheòil;
Nuair bhithinn 'm ònar, 's mi fo ghruaim,
'S mo bhuadhan gun chus treòir,
Cha b' fhada mulad teicheadh bhuam
Am measg nan *Sguaban Eòrn'*.

Is iomadh eachdraidh rinn thu inns'
'S a sgrìobh thu dhuinn le deòin
Le ealantachd a thug dhuit buaidh
Is duais aig iomadh Mòd;
Cha d' dh'fhàg thu 'n easbhaidh tìr nam beann,
Thug thu dhi fuinn is ceòl,
Thug thu an crùn a-nall bharr chuain —
Is sgrìobh thu *Sguaban Eòrn'*.

Dh'inn's thu dhuinn mu ànradh cruaidh
Do chuairt anns an Roinn Eòrp'
Fo bhinn an lasair, is an luaidh,
Is iomadh cruas den t-seòrs',
Am prìosan cogaidh glaiste suas
Cho fad' bho d' dhual is d' eòl,
Cho fad' bho eilean beag a' chuain
'S cho fad' bho bhruaich na Cròic'.

Sgrìobh thu ann am briathran blàth
Mu mhaise 's gràdh nan òigh,
Mhol thu Mòrag dhonn nan dual
Is buadhan Maighread Òig;
Le eireachdas is loinn o d' pheann,
Le còmhradh, cainnt is ceòl
Thog thu suas air stìopall àrd
Taigh a' bhàird nach beò.

The Poet

I salute you, poet friend,
And most willingly shake hands —
You often raised my mind aloft
With the talents of your mouth;
When alone, and feeling low,
My powers without much strength,
My sadness would not last for long
Amongst the *Barley Sheaves*.[1]

Many stories have you told us
And gladly written down
With skill that's brought you much success
And prizes at the Mòd;
You have enhanced our mountain land,
And given her airs and music,
You brought the crown across the Minch —
And wrote the *Barley Sheaves*.

You told us of the dreadful trials
Which you experienced in Europe,
Enduring cruelty, flames of wrath,
And many hardships of that kind,
In prison camp locked up so far
From all you knew and loved,
From the little island of the sea
And from the brae of the Cròic.[2]

In warm words you wrote of the beauty
And of the love of the girls,
You praised Mòrag of the auburn locks
And the charms of Maighread Òg;[3]
With your pen's skill and eloquence,
With music, dialogue and speech
You raised on high upon a tower
The house of the late poet.[4]

Guma fad' thu fallain buan
  An eilean uaine d' òig',
Ag àiteach fuinn, a' cur, 's a' buain,
  'S a' ceangal sguaban eòrn',
A' sgrìobhadh bàrdachd agus duain
  Bha dualach dhuit o d' òig,
'S gu h-inntinneach a' gabhail cuairt
  Mu bhruaichean Tràigh na Cròic'.

An Rocaid

'Na mo shuidhe ann an cùil chumhaing
aig mullach rocaid,
dithis chompanach còmhla rium
ag éisteachd, cunntais —
deich, naoi, h-ochd —
mo chridhe plapadaich ag éisteachd —
seachd, sia, cóig —
m' inntinn, a shiùbhlas nas luaithe na solas,
air a' ghealaich romham;
mi fàgail an t-saoghail, 's mi 'n dùil ri tilleadh —
ceithir, trì, dhà, aon —
lasadh:
dhealaich mi ris an talamh,
cumhachd a thugadh ás an t-saoghal
gam thogail bhon t-saoghal.

Cruth m' aodainn ag atharrachadh,
an saoghal ga mo tharraing air n-ais thuige,
ach thug cumhachd beag ann an acfhainn
buaidh air cumhachd mór a bha sgaoilte;
dhealaich mi gu tur ris an talamh,
tha mi siubhal luath agus a' fàs beagan nas òige.

Tha mi a' cadal agus a' dùsgadh,
ithidh mi biadh agus chan eil cuideam annam,
seòlaidh mi 'na mo sheòmar
mar fhaoileag air sgéith,

May you live a long and healthy life
In the green isle of your youth,
Tilling land, sowing, reaping,
And binding barley sheaves,
Writing down the poems and songs
That were in your blood from childhood,
And going out for pleasant walks
Round the braes of Tràigh na Cròice.

The Rocket

Sitting in a narrow cockpit
at the top of a rocket,
two colleagues along with me
listening, counting —
ten, nine, eight —
my heart thumping as I listen —
seven, six, five —
my mind, which travels faster than light,
on the moon before me;
while leaving the world, I expect to return —
four, three, two, one —
ignition:
I've parted from the earth,
a power taken from the world
lifting me from the world.

My face's shape being distorted,
the world pulling me back to itself,
But small power in harness
has beaten big power unharnessed;
I've parted fully with the earth,
I'm travelling fast and growing a little younger.

I fall asleep and wake up,
I eat some food and am weightless,
I glide in my chamber
like a gull on the wing,

tha mi a' cuartachadh na gealaich
's air mo tharraing ga h-ionnsaigh;
chì mi taobh dhith nach fhaca mi riamh.

Fàgaidh sinn companach ga cuartachadh,
tha mi fhìn agus fear eile dol sìos;
laigh sinn mar iolaire
agus se sin a thubhairt sinn:
"Tha sinn ann a-seo, dithis bheò
ann am fàsach mór marbh."
Tha sinn a' bocadaich mun cuairt
eadar bhith coiseachd 's a bhith seòladh,
tha 'n saoghal mar ghealaich mhóir liath
ag éirigh suas,
sealladh nach tuig inntinn
ach am fear a bh' ann
's a chunnaic.

Anail na beatha air mo dhruim
's chì mi liath i air astar,
cluinnidh sibh agus chì sibh mi
le innleachd dhaoine
's mi ag éirigh tro speuran na gealaich.
Tha an triùir againn còmhla gu dòigheil a-rithist,
a' feuchainn dhachaigh
's a' dol tron chachaileith chumhaing;
tha sinn innte, cha chluinn sinn dad
agus cha chluinn duine sinne,
teas mór thar tomhais a' leaghadh
taobh a-muigh ar taigh-còmhnaidh,
ach tha e nis air fuarachadh sa chuan.

Tha sinn air tilleadh air n-ais,
tha sinn gu math,
ach cha bhi sinn tuilleadh mar a bha sinn.

I'm orbiting the moon
and being pulled towards it;
I see a side of it I've never seen.

We leave a colleague in orbit,
another man and I are going down;
like an eagle we've landed
and this is what we said:
"We're here, two of us alive
in a great lifeless wilderness."
We're bouncing around
halfway between walking and flying,
the world's like a great pale-blue moon
rising up,
a sight no mind can imagine
except the man who was there
and who saw.

With the breath of life on my back
I see it pale-blue afar,
you all hear me and see me
by man's ingenuity
as I rise through the skies of the moon.
We three are safely together again,
heading for home
and going through the narrow gate;
we're aboard, we hear nothing
and nobody hears us,
a great immeasurable heat melting
the outside of our dwelling-house,
but it's now cooled down in the ocean.

We have come back,
we are all right,
but we'll be no more as we were.

An t-Eun Fuadain

Chan i seo an dùthaich dha'n dùthchas dhut bhith tàmh:
Chuir stoirm is gailleann faoiltich thu air faondradh thar an t-sàil;
Dh'fhàg thu cridhe brùit' againn thu dhol a-null cho tràth
A dh'ainneoin ar cuid cungaisich, cha d' chum sinn thu bhon bhàs.

Tha itean bòidheach ciatach ort cho dubh ri fiamh na teàrr
Is broilleach mar an sneachda bhios 'na stac air feadh nan càrn;
Tha spògan beaga rìomhach ort cho mìn ri canach blàir
Is dhearbh iad dha mo shùilean gum bu dùthchas dhut bhith snàmh.

Rinn mi uaigh bhòidheach dhut bho fhòirneart air do dhìon
Is rinn mi ùrnaigh shoisgealach, oir toil leam ceòl nan ian;
Nuair thig an latha sònraichte chaidh òrdachadh le Dia,
Bidh thusa snàmh gu sòlasach air bòc-thuinn a' Chuain Siar.

Cha Mhór tha ri Àireamh

Cha mhór tha ri àireamh dhe m' luchd eòlais san àite,
Tha iad shìos ann an t-Hàllann a' cnàmh fo na fòid;
Cha chluinn iad a' ghàirich aig tuinn Lag an t-Sàile
'S chan fhaic iad na crà-gheòidh a' snàmh anns an òb.

Sa mhadainn cha dùisg iad le aiteas no sùgradh
Fo ghlasan nach mùth ann an duirche nam bòrd;
Cha treabh iad a' bhuaile, chan àitich 's cha bhuain iad —
Thàinig deireadh an cuairt ann an cluaintean nam beò.

Cha téid iad gu sàile ri lìonadh no tràghadh,
Cha chuir iad gu bràch crann bàt' ann am bròig,
Cha cheangail 's chan fhuasgail iad ròpa na cruaidh-shnaidhm,
Chan iomair chun an fhuaraidh 's cha chruadhaich a seòl.

Bu chridheil am mànran nuair bhiodh iad mun cheàrdaich
A' deasbad mu chàirdeas 's mu ghnàthachd an òig',
Bhiodh Niall Mhurchaidh a' fàsgadh na builg gu làidir —
S iomadh coltair 's crann-arain chaidh a thàthadh le mheòir.

The Stray Bird

This is not the country where it's in your blood to stay:
Storm and wolftime gale have sent you off your ocean's course;
You've left us broken-hearted that you passed away so soon
Despite all our attempts to help, we failed to keep you from death.

You have fine and splendid feathers as black in hue as tar
And a breast like the snow that piles up on rock-strewn slopes;
You have lovely little talons as smooth as cotton in the marsh
And they have proven to my eyes that swimming's in your blood.

I've made a lovely grave for you to save you from attack
And I've said a prayer from the gospel, for I love the music of birds;
When it comes to that special day which God has ordained,
You'll be swimming happily on the great Atlantic waves.

Not Many are Left

Not many are left of my friends in the district,
They're down in Hallin rotting under the sods;
They can't hear the roaring of waves in the Inlet
And can't see the shelduck swim in the creek.

Under unchanging locks in the dark of the coffin
They can't wake in the morning with joy or delight;
They can't till the field, they can't plough or harvest —
They've reached the end of their trip to the lawns of this life.

They can't go to sea at the fill or the ebb-tide,
They'll never put boat's mast into its shoe,
They can't fasten or loosen the tight-knotted rope,
They can't row to windward and her sail will not fill.

Bright was their banter round the door of the smithy
Discussing relationships and pranks from their youth,
Niall Mhurchaidh manfully squeezing the bellows —
Many coulters and ploughs were joined by his fingers.

Sa gheamhradh gum b' éibhinn bhith triall don taigh-chéilidh
Far an cluinneamaid sgeul ris an éisteadh gach seòrs' —
Bhiodh snìomh agus càrdadh, bhiodh lìn ann ri'n càradh
'S bhiodh ìm agus càis' air a chàrnadh air bòrd.

Se bodaich bhiodh sunndach a' froiseadh 's a' sùisteadh,
Cha bhiodh gruaim air an gnùis, bha iad sùrdalach, beò;
Cha leigeadh iad mùigeachd bhith riaghladh an cùrsa
'S bhiodh balgam sa chùil ac' de shùgh blast' an eòrn'.

Bu tric a' gluasad a-mach feadh nan cruaidh-chnoc
Far am biodh iad a' ruamhar gu buannachd an lòin —
A' bristeadh, 's a' taomadh, is feamainn ga sgaoileadh,
Cha robh cobhair ri fhaotainn ach saothair nan dòrn.

Dh'fhalbh iad 's cha till iad gu bràch do na glinn seo,
Ann an suaimhneas na sìth tha iad sìnte fon fhòd;
Ged nach d' mheal iad cus saorsa 'nan cuairt anns an t-saoghal
Cha bhi cìsean cho daor dol troimh chaolais na Glòir.

Caochladh

Tha m' inntinn trom, gun sunnd, gun fhonn,
Cha bhrosnaich pong ceòl mi,
Le ceuman mall a' ruith mo réis
Gu oirthir chéin nach eòl dhomh.

Rinn m' earrach ùr-bhlàth ruith gu cheann
Is thriall mo shamhradh òr-bhuidh';
Tha deireadh m' fhoghair tighinn gu luath
'S tha geamhradh fuar 'nam sheòmar.

Chan fhaic mi dìtheanan air bruaich,
Chan fhaic mi snuadh nan ròsan;
Cha léir dhomh nis ach aogais fhuar
Far 'm faicinn uair a' bhòidhchead.

It was pleasant in winter to go to the ceilidh-house
  Where we'd hear a tale to which all sorts would listen —
There'd be spinning and carding, and nets to repair,
  With butter and cheese heaped up on a table.

Old fellows were merry when threshing and flailing,
  With no girn on their faces, energetic, alive;
They'd never let grumpiness rule their activities
  And they'd have a drop tucked away of the best barley bree.

Frequently walking out over the rocky hills
  Where they'd be digging to grow themselves food —
Breaking soil, planting, and spreading the seaweed,
  With no help to be had but the toil of their fists.

They've gone and will never return to these glens,
  In the silence of peace they lie under the sod;
They enjoyed little freedom in their stay in the world
  But tolls won't be so high going through Heaven's kyles.

Change

My mind is heavy, cheerless, tuneless,
  No note of music lifts me,
Running my race with steps that are slow
  To a distant shore unknown.

My fresh-blossomed spring has run its course
  And my bright golden summer has gone;
The end of my autumn's coming quickly
  And cold winter's in my room.

I see no flowers upon a slope,
  Nor do I see the roses' hue;
All I can see now are spectres of cold
  Where once I could see great beauty.

Tha dorchadas a' tarraing dlùth
  Bhon dh'imrich mùirn na h-òige,
Tha srann a' cheàrdubhain 'nam chluais
  Cur smaoin na truaigh' 'nam dhòchas.

Tha gleann an àigh far 'n d'fhàs mi suas
  Fo luachair is fo chòinnich —
Tha caochladh air tighinn air a shnuadh
  Bhon dh'fhalbh an sluagh a b' eòl dhomh.

Bidh guileag eala bhàin air cuan,
  Bidh guth na cuaich' san Ògmhios,
Ach bidh na cagailtean cho fuar
  Ri sneachd on tuath a' còpadh.

Bidh buairidhean is beachdan faoin'
  Gar toirt a thaobh le seòltachd,
A' gealltainn lùchairtean an seud,
  'S gach duais air mheud an òr-mheinn.

Ged s beag de thuigse tha 'nam cheann
  Gun inn's an gleann gu leòr dhomh,
'S gun dèan e thaisbean dhomh gu luath
  Gum faigh an uaigh a còirean.

Tha eachdraidh anns na taighean fàs
  'S beachd-smaointeachadh ri fheòrach
Gu eadar-theangachadh mo sgeul
  Ma théid a leughadh dòigheil.

Chan eil e 'n comas chlann nan daoin'
  An t-aog a chur air fògradh;
Ged fhuair sinn cead ar toil gu saor
  Tha crìoch ar saoghail òrdaicht'

Darkness has been coming close
Since the joy of youth receded,
The beetle's hum is in my ear
Filling hope with wretched thoughts.

The glorious glen where I grew up
Is under rushes and moss —
A change came on its hue
When the folk I knew went off.

The white swan will sing upon the sea,
The cuckoo will be heard in June,
But the hearthstones will have turned as cold
As a blizzard blowing from the north.

Temptations and false opinions
Will cunningly deflect us,
Promising their jewelled palaces,
Each prize the size of a goldmine.

Though I've little smartness in my head
The glen can tell me plenty,
It can speedily reveal to me
That the grave will have its due.

History's in the empty houses
And an idea's to be pursued
For the translation of my tale
If it's read as it ought to be.

It's not in human competence
To send death to banishment;
Though we got the gift of our free will
Our life's conclusion is ordained.

Cha Till an Òige

Tillidh, tillidh am muir-làn
Tacan beag as déidh muir-tràigh:
Lìonar leis air ais na bàigh,
    Ach gu bràch cha till an òig'.
Tillidh, tillidh am muir-làn.

Tillidh earrach grianach blàth,
Théid an sìol a chur san ùir,
Ceòl na cubhaig' feadh nan stùc
    Mar as dùthchas san t-seann nòs.
Tillidh, tillidh am muir-làn.

Tillidh samhradh ruinn le sunnd
'S bidh na machraichean fo bhàrr —
Coirce 's eòrna mar as àill
    'S gucag a' bhuntàt' as bòidhch'.
Tillidh, tillidh am muir-làn.

Tillidh foghar ruinn mun cuairt,
Bidh luchd fearainn trang a' buain,
Fear na speal' le buille chruaidh
    Toirt nan dias a-nuas 'nan dlòth.
Tillidh, tillidh am muir-làn.

Tillidh geamhradh mar as dual
Le chuid sneachda 's gaoth a-tuath,
Na h-eich bhàn' air bhàrr a' chuain
    Tighinn le nuallan chun a' chòrs.
Tillidh, tillidh am muir-làn.

Eachdraidh sgrìobhadair bho chian,
Tha e dearbht' gu bheil i fìor —
Leis a-sin bidh sinne triall
    Tarsainn crìochan gleann nan deòir.
Tillidh, tillidh am muir-làn.

Youth will not Return

High tide will return, return,
A short while after ebbing:
It will fill the bays again,
    But never will our youth return.
High tide will return, return.

Warm sunny spring will return,
The seed will be sown in the soil,
The cuckoo'll sing among the crags
    As is normal in old verse.
High tide will return, return.

Summer will return with cheer
And crops will grow in machairlands —
Oats and barley as desired
    And the loveliest potato bloom.
High tide will return, return.

Harvest will come back around,
Country people busy reaping,
The scyther with a mighty stroke
    Bringing down the ears in sheaves.
High tide will return, return.

Winter will come back as always
With its northerlies and snow,
White horses on the ocean's crest
    Roaring in towards the shore.
High tide will return, return.

History written long ago,
It's proven to be true —
Thus it is that we'll travel
    Over the bounds of the valley of tears.
High tide will return, return.

Bhon as coigrich sinn air chuairt
Tha sinn cinnteach ás ar duais:
Léine anairt 's bòrdan cruaidh
'S dol air uachdar sin bidh 'm fòd.
Tillidh, tillidh am muir-làn.

Gheibh sinn sàmhchair anns an uaigh,
Sìochaint sìth na dachaigh bhuain
Gus an séid an trombaid shuas
Air son ar gluasad chun a' mhòid.
Tillidh, tillidh am muir-làn.

Tillidh, tillidh am muir-làn
Tacan beag as déidh muir-tràigh:
Lìonar leis air ais na bàigh,
Ach gu bràch cha till an òig'.
Tillidh, tillidh am muir-làn.

Bàgh Hartabhagh

Ma bheir tachartas gu bràth
Thu don àit' seo air chuairt,
Chì thu seallaidhean le d' shùil
A bheir ùrachd dha d' smuain.

Chì thu monaidhean fo fhraoch
Fàs 'na chraobhagan uain'
'S chì thu blianagan as bòidhch'
Air an òradh le snuadh.

Chì thu tobraichean tha fàs
Agus làraichean fuar
A' toirt breithneachadh nach gann
Air an àm chaidh air ruaig.

Chì thu cuimhneachain gu leòr
'S gheibh thu eòlas as ùr —
Bidh na h-eachdraidhean gu léir
Tighinn cho réidh gu do shùil.

Since we're strangers on a tour
We can be sure of our reward:
Linen shroud and wooden boards
    With sods of turf upon the top.
High tide will return, return.

We'll find silence in the grave,
Peaceful rest of home forever
Till the trumpet sounds on high
    To summon us to judgement.
High tide will return, return.

High tide will return, return,
A short while after ebbing:
It will fill the bays again,
    But never will our youth return.
High tide will return, return.

Hartavagh Bay

If life ever happens to bring you
  To this place on a visit,
You'll see sights with your eye
  To stimulate your thoughts.

You'll see moors under heather
  Growing in little green tree-shapes
While the loveliest of lawns
  Are changed to gold in colour.

You'll see wells that are deserted
  And the cold sites of houses
Providing evidence galore
  Of a time that's gone by.

You'll see memories aplenty
  And get knowledge that's new —
All histories will come
  So neatly to your view.

Chì thu buailtean a' chruidh-laoigh
Air gach taobh anns a' ghleann
A' toirt taisbean le'n cuid sgeul
Air na treun-fhir a bh' ann.

Chì thu cairidhean sa bhàgh,
Saothair làmhan bha cruaidh,
Seòltachd gu glacadh éisg
Dearbhadh ainbheirt an t-sluaigh.

Chì thu calmain agus naoisg,
Cearcan-fraoich agus geòidh,
Gearradh-breac a' snàmh nan tonn
'S dreathan-donn feadh nan còs.

Chì thu iolaire nan spòg
'S fiamh an òir dhith san speur —
Sann an uaigneas bhios a tàmh
Shuas air àird Sgòrr an Fhéidh.

Maise nàdair air gach taobh,
Sìth is caoineas mun cuairt,
Sàmhchair àrsaidh gun fhiamh —
Raghadh iarratais sluaigh.

Còmhradh an Eilthirich ris an Stuaidh

Ma ruigeas tu Eilean Uibhist
Air do thuras troimhn a' chuan,
Buailidh tu air cladach m' òige
Far am b' eòlach bha mi uair.

Nuair a ruigeas tu an tràigh ann
Bidh ghaineamh bhàn ri oir na tìr';
Chì thu làrach mo dhà shàil ann
Mur do dh'fhàilig iad ri tìm.

You'll see the folds of the milk-cows
  On each side of the glen
Giving witness by their stories
  To the heroes that were there.

You'll see weirs in the bay,
  Work of hands that was hard,
A device to catch fish
  That shows people's plight.

You'll see doves, you'll see snipe,
  You'll see moorhens and geese,
The guillemot who swims the waves
  And the wren who lives in holes.

You'll see the taloned eagle
  Gleaming gold in the skies —
In isolation she dwells
  Up high on Sgòrr an Fhéidh.

Nature's beauty on all sides,
  Peace and gentleness all round,
Ancient silence without fear —
  What people like the best.

Conversation between an Emigrant and a Wave

If you reach the Isle of Uist
  On your journey through the sea,
You will hit the shore of my boyhood
  Which I knew so well at one time.

When you reach the sea shore
  The white sand will be on the edge of the land;
You will find there my footprints
  Unless they have failed through time.

Nuair a bha mi òg 'nam shealgair
Bu tric mi falbh air feadh nam bàgh;
S pailt mo lorg air feadh nan garbhlach
Far an dèan na calmain tàmh.

Ma bhuaileas tu aig Lag an t-Sàile
Gum bi sàmhchair ort mun cuairt;
Sann an sìochaint sìth Chnoc Hàllainn
Tha mo chàirdean-sa 'nan suain.

Tha mo chàirdean 's mo luchd-eòlais
Fo na fòidean ann a' cnàmh;
Sann 'nam measg bu mhiann mo chòmhnaidh
Nuair nì mi còmhdhail ris a' bhàs.

An t-eilean grianach rinn mi fhàgail,
Thoir mìle fàilte dha le spéis;
Is ann a dh'iarrainn a bhith tàmhachd
Seach aon àite tha fon a' ghréin.

Ged a thug mi ris mo chùlaibh
Bidh mo dhùrachd ann gu bràch,
'S bidh mo bheannachdan ga ionnsaigh
Air an dùblachadh le bàidh.

Chi thu Éiseabhal nan stùcan
Le cuid chùiltean agus chàrn;
S tric a dealbh a' tighinn 'nam inntinn
Bhon a dh'imrich mi thar sàl.

Chì thu 'n tìr a dh'àraich òg mi
Sgèimhichte le cleòc as àill —
Seagal, coirce agus eòrna
'S gucag bhòidheach a' bhuntàt'.

S iomadh smuain a bhios gam dhealgadh
'S mi fad air falbh bho eilean m' òig',
Fad bho eilean gorm mo dhùthchais
Far an lùiginn a bhith beò.

When I was a young hunter
  I used to wander around the bays;
My footsteps can be traced
  Where the dove makes his abode.

If you hit the Cavity of the Salt Water
  There will be silence all around;
In the tranquillity of Hallan cemetery
  My relations sleep sound.

My friends and relations
  Are decaying under the turf;
My desire is to be among them
  When my eyes close in death.

The sunny island which I left,
  Give it my welcome and love;
Of all the places under the sun
  There's where I would like to stay.

Although I left it behind me
  My goodwill is always there;
My blessings will always reach towards it
  And they are doubled with love.

You will see Eiseabhal of the glens
  With its hollows and dales;
Its image is always on my mind
  Since I moved across the sea.

You will see the land which reared me when young,
  Its green crop growing to harvest —
Rye, oats and barley
  And the lovely bud on the potatoes.

Many a thought passes through my mind
  Far away from the land of my youth,
Far from the land of my birth
  Where I always desire to be.

Thoir mo shoraidh do gach nàbaidh
Rinn mi fhàgail as mo dhéidh —
Gheibh iad ann an cop an t-sàile
Aithris bhlàth bhon dùthaich chéin.

Cumha

Nuair chaislich gaoth a' Chéitein bàrr nam flùran
Bha aoibh is gaol is sùgradh ann an còmhradh,
Bha briathran geallaidh caomhalachd ri'n éisteachd
'S bha uaimeachd eadar eud is mullach dòchais.

Thig oiteag bhlàth thar bhàrr nan tonnan uaine
A' dùsgadh smuaintean 's a toirt bruadar bèo dhuinn,
A' dearbhadh dhuinn cho aithghearr 's a tha 'n ùine
Bhon bha Faoilteach dùr toirt fùcadh treòir oirnn.

Thug an Céitean dhuinn air ais na flùran
'S thug e bhuainn an t-ùr-blàth 's robh 'bhòidhche;
Aig ceithir deug a bhliadhachan de dh'ùine
Gur duilich leam an ùir a bhith gad chòmhdach.

S duilich leam do chuailean dualach rìomhach
A bhith ann an ionad anns nach cuir a' chìr air dòigh e;
Nì mi dealbh na h-àilleachd anns an ùir dhiot
Ged nach faca mi le m' shùilean anns an fheòil thu.

Dh'fhàg thu as do dhéidh an saoghal gruamach
Nach robh aoigheil riut no suairc nuair bha thu bèo ann;
Ghabh thu t' aiseag chun a' chala shàbhailt'
Far 'm bi thu ann an càirdeas feachd na glòrach.

Bidh crònan tonnan iargail Lag an t-Sàile
A' brosnachadh nan tàlaidh is nan ceòl-bhinn;
Bidh rùin phàirtichte do chàirdean mun an uain'-chnoc
'S bidh cuimhneachain bhios buan far 'n deach an òige.

Take my blessings to my neighbours
Whom I have left behind —
They will receive in the foam of the ocean
A warm remembrance from the foreign land.

(*author's translation*)

Lament

When the winds of May rustled through the flowers
There was courtesy and love in their conversation,
There was mildness and mirth in the language
Forming a boundary between jealousy and hope.

The fresh wind blowing from the ocean
Awakening our thoughts and reviving our dreams,
Brings home to us how short the space of time
Since stubborn January showed its hatred.

The month of May brought back the flowers
But it took away the fruitful blossom;
At fourteen years of age
It's sad that wood and sand are your garments.

It's sad that your beautiful curly hair
Is in a state where the comb can't put it in order;
I can picture your handsome features in the grave
Although I never saw you in the flesh.

You left behind the gloomy world
Which was not kind and meek to you when living;
You made the journey to the safe harbour
Where you will be in the company of heavenly angels.

The soft murmur of the ocean on the shoreline
Will provide the music and the lullaby;
The communicating of your relations will be around the green hillock
And everlasting memory round the grave of the young.

Is iomadh madainn Chéitein a nì ùislinn
  Is gaoth a' caisleadh fhlùran a bhios òrail
Air uachdar an t-seòmair chadail anns nach dùisg sinn
  Nuair chuireas làmhan chàich na bùird gar còmhdach.

Dealbh Camilla

Chunnaic mi do dhealbh mar òr-sheud
Am pàipear *Posta Di-Dòmhnaich*
Mar reul iùil do dh'fhear an t-seòlaidh
  Bhios air bhòidse fad' bho thìr.

Chunnaic mise dealbh na h-àilleachd,
Rìbhinn ghrinn a' chuailein fhàinnich,
Marcachd steud air achadh fàschoill —
  Ìomhaigh fhàilteach agus sìth.

Aodann aoibhnis choibhneil chàirdeil,
Dreach do ghnùis mar ubhal an gàrradh;
Deud cho geal ri sneachd air àrd-bheinn
  'S cathadh-làir air ùrlar glinn.

Tha do shùilean ann am bòidhche
Mar an dealt air bhàrr nan neòinean;
Calpa cuimir is troigh chòmhnard —
  Cha do sheas am bròig cho grinn.

Ged a mharcaich thu na leòidean
'S air raointean farsaing tha d' mhion-eòlais,
Cha do smaointich thu 'nad òige
  D' ainm bhith 'm meòmhair anns na glinn.

Cha do dh'aisling thu air cluasaig
'S cha do bhrist e steach 'nad smuaintean
Gum biodh do dhealbh ann cho luachmhor
  Am measg ghleanntan uain' an fhraoich.

Many are the May mornings in wantonness
    The wind will rustle the gilding flowers
Over the apartment from which we shall not awaken
    When the hands of other people have put the boards on us as covering.

(author's translation)

Camilla's Picture

I saw your picture like a golden jewel
In the paper *Sunday Post*
Like a guiding star to the mariner
        On a voyage far from land.

I saw the picture of beauty,
Handsome lady of the golden tresses,
Mounting a steed on a green field —
        The image of peace and welcome.

A face of joy and friendship,
The hue of your complexion is like an apple in a garden;
Your teeth as white as snow on a mountain
        And ground drift on the floor of a glen.

The beauty of your eyes
Resembles the dew on a daisy;
The calves of your legs are attractive and elegant —
        As graceful as stood inside a shoe.

Although you rode on many fields
And of wide plains you have vast knowledge,
You never thought in your younger days
        Your name would be remembered in the glens.

You never dreamed on your pillow
And it never entered your mind
That your picture would be so treasured
        Among the green heathery glens.

(author's translation)

Don Bhean Phòsta Jacqueline Marsh

Mar éirigh gréin' air madainn bhòidheach samhraidh
Tha gaol gun chaochladh a' deàlradh ann ad' ghnùis;
Mar ghealach làn air oidhche reòdhta geamhraidh
Tha loinn a' boillsgeadh coibhnis 'nad dhà shùil.

Mar laigheas driùchd air duilleach grinn an neòinein
Mun seinn a' chòisridh cheòlmhor anns an àird',
Bidh aoibh is sonas far am bi do chòmhnaidh
'S bidh carthannachd mar chòmhdach dhut gu bràch.

Cho abaich ris na diasan anns an t-Sultuin
Tha dreach nan ròsan ruiteach tha 'nad ghruaidh;
Tha t' anail measgaichte le mil nam flùran
Fo bhlàth le duilleach ùr air feadh nan cluain.

Cho ealanta ri salmadair nan sgiathan
A sheinneas dhuinn cho ciatach anns a' Mhàigh,
Cho dealbhach ri Bhénus anns an iarmailt
Tha rìbhinn ghrinn na tìoralachd 's na bàidh.

Do Mhàiri NicillEathain, Griomsaigh

Fàilt', a ghruagach dhonn mo ghaoil,
Si d' aoibh a thog mo cheòl
'S a chuireadh sunnd 'nam chom le gaol
'S a dh'aotromaich mo bhròn;
Ged bhithinn ìosal iomadh uair
Mar as dualach do mo sheòrs',
Nì fiamh do ghàire blàths do m' chrìdh
'S do bhrìodal m' fhàgail òg.

An dealbh a nì mi dhiot an-dràst'
Mar eala snàmh san òb,
Mar shneachd air mullach nam beann àrd
'S e deàrrsadh madainn reòdht',

Mrs Jacqueline Marsh

Like the rising of the sun on a lovely summer morning
    There is love which does not alter in your face;
Like a full moon on a frosty winter night
    Beauty is shining in your eyes.

As the dew subsides on the elegant leaves of the daisy
    Before the birds start singing in the sky,
There will be charm and prosperity in your dwelling
    And charity will surround you all your life.

As the ripeness of the corn in September
    Is the appearance of your red rosy cheeks;
Your breath is mingled with the honey of flowers
    Under the new blossom among the green fields.

As melodious as the birds of the firmament
    That will sing so sweetly as they sway,
As handsome as Venus in the Heavens
    Is the elegant lady of the warmth and the love.

(*author's translation*)

To Mary Maclean, Grimsay

Greetings, my darling brownhaired lass,
    Your charm's set me composing
For it's always brightened my soul with love
    And lightened my depression;
Though time and again I have been low
    As my kind is inclined to be,
The sight of your smile brings warmth to my heart
    While your banter restores my youth.

The image I'll make of you just now
    Is of a swan that swims in the bay,
Of snow on the highest mountain tops
    As it gleams in the morning frost,

Mar long fo shiùil a-muigh sa chuan
'S a' ghaoth cho cruaidh gu còrs',
'S i stiùireadh cùrsa nall gu luath
Gu Uibhist uain' an eòrn'.

Mar ghathan gréin' san àird' an-iar
Tha ìomhaigh chiùin na h-òigh',
Tha blàths is càirdeas, agus rian,
Tha Crìostalachd 'nad fheòil;
Tha àilleachd a' snàmh 'nad ghnùis —
Gach seòrsa flùir as bòidhch',
Tha ròsan 's ùbhlan 'na do ghruaidh
'S céir-bheach mun cuairt do bheòil.

Cridhe coibhneil agus blàth
Cur fàilt' air aois is òig',
Bidh beannachd dhaoine leat gu bràth
Gach là fhads bhios tu beò;
Gur fhad o chuireadh ort an crùn
Gu mùirneach aig a' Mhòd
'S a fhuair thu 'n t-urram bhith 'nad Bhàrd
Le tàlantan do bheòil!

Nuair thig ciaradh air mo là
Is gath a' bhàis 'nam fheòil,
A' dol don t-sìorraidheachd gu bràth
'S a' laigh' a' cnàmh fon fhòd,
Mhiannaichinn gum bithinn dlùth
Don mhaighdinn rùnaich chòir
Ris an robh mi réidh o thùs —
'S cha bhrist an ùir an còrd.

Fàilt' an t-Sagairt Òig

Mìle fàilt' oirbh a Chrìostaidh 's beannachd Dhia bhith 'nur comhair:
Guma fada sibh 'nur buachaill a' cumail sluaigh ann an dòchas;
Beannachd Dhé agus dhaoine bhith dhuibh daonnan mar lòchran —
'S naomh Peadair 'nur càirdeas a h-uile là fhads as beò sibh.

Of a ship in full sail out there in the ocean
While the wind blows hard to the shore,
Steering her course so swiftly across
To pale-green Uist of the barley.

Like rays of sunshine in the west
Is the girl's serene appearance,
There's warmth and friendship, and self-possession,
There's Christianity in your flesh;
There's beauty swimming in your face —
Each kind of flower that's loveliest,
Roses and apples are in your cheek
And beeswax around your mouth.

A heart that's full of warmth and kindness
Welcoming both old and young,
People's blessings go with you forever
Each day that you're alive;
O how long it is since you were crowned
Ceremonially at the Mòd
And received the honour of being Bard
For the talents of your mouth!

When evening descends upon my day
With the dart of death in my flesh,
Going for all time to eternity
And lying rotting in the soil,
I'd wish forever to be close
To the girl who's dear and kind
And who has always been my friend —
And the grave won't break the cord.

The Young Priest's Welcome

A thousand welcomes servant of God and may his blessings be always with you:
Long may you be his shepherd keeping watch over his flock;
May the blessings of God be always your guiding star —
And may Saint Peter be your companion all the days of your life.

(*author's translation)*

Don Té Rinn Tighinn gam Fheòraich Dhachaigh

Don Mhnaoi Phòsta Catrìona Laing, Uibhist a-Tuath, ceannard seirbheis cobhair na dachaigh

Bhon tha peann agam 'nam mheòirean,
Sgrìobhaidh mi leis sìos mun t-sòlas
Rinn mi ris an rìbhinn bhòidhich
A thàinig gam fheòraich dhachaigh.

Tha i laghach agus bàidheil,
Air a h-aodann fiamh a' ghàire;
Tha h-anail mar ghaoth a' ghàrraidh
Far am fàs na blàthan fallain.

Tha i coingeis Beur' no Gàidhlig,
Tha i comasach sna dhà dhiubh;
Bhuilich freastal oirre tàlann
A thug àrd i ann an aithne.

Tha i tapaidh agus sunndach,
Deas 'na pearsa 's 'na giùlan;
A dà ghruaidh air dhreach nan ùbhlan
Bhios air cunntair bùth a' cheannaich'.

Tha i leam mar reul san iarmailt
An àm don fheasgar a bhith ciaradh,
An uair tha ghrian a' cromadh sìos
'S an cuan an-iar a' dol ga falach.

Tha a brìodal leam cho ceòlmhor
Ri pìob-mhàl' fo raghadh mheòirean;
Tha a crìdh cho làn de chòiread —
Cha dèan mèinn an òir a cheannach.

Tha de thaitneas 'na briathran
Na chuireadh mì-ghean air dìochuimhn',
Tha deud cho geal ri sneachd' air sliabh
'S e measgaichte le trian clach-mheallain.

In Praise of the Lady who Came Home to See Me

To Mrs Cathy Laing, North Uist, head of the home help service

As it happens that I have the pen in my fingers,
I will write down with pleasure
About the beautiful lady
Who came home to see me.

She is nice and pretty,
And on her face a lovely smile;
Her breath is like the freshness
Coming from a garden of flowers.

She can talk English and Gaelic,
She is fluent in both languages;
She is blessed with talents
Which brought her to high office.

She is strong and healthy,
Fit in mind and body;
Her cheeks are as rosy
As apples on the counter of a merchant's shop.

I see her as a star in the Heavens
When darkness falls,
When the sun is declining
And the ocean going to hide her from our view.

Her speech is as musical as the bagpipes
Played by elegant fingers;
Her heart is full of kindness —
A gold mine could never buy it.

Her voice is so pleasing
It will cast gloom away,
Her teeth as white as snow and hail
Mixed in the drifts of a field.

Falt dubh dualach ann an òrdagh
'S e cho snuadhmhor agus bòidheach:
Chan eil teagamh nach do chòrd sinn,
Chuir i sòlas mun a' chagailt.

Sgaoil ar conaltradh gu làidir:
Bhruidhinn sinn mu iomadh àite
Eadar sgòrr-bheanntan Chinn t-Sàile
Chun a' chàirn a th' air Beinn Bhragaidh.

Nuair a dh'fhalbh i bha mi tùrsach,
Tha mi daonnan ann ga h-ionndrainn:
Tha h-ìomhaigh leam a-cheart cho rùnach
Ris na flùran air a' mhachair.

Bidh mo bheannachd ga còmhdhail
Anns an àit' sam bheil i còmhnaidh —
Cadal suaimhneach socair stòlda
'S dùsgadh beòthail anns a' mhadainn.

Eich Éirisgeigh

Bha iad riamh an Éirisgeigh 's gum b' fheumail iad don t-sluagh,
Bha iad troimh na linntean ann sna tìmean chaidh air ruaig;
Thàirneadh iad a' mhòine gu fògairt chur air fuachd
Is làimhsicheadh an òigridh iad 's bha iomadh spòrs 'nan cuairt.

Gu toirt todhar far na tràghad bha iad làidir agus treun,
Bheireadh iad gun spàirn an àirde paidhir chléibh;
Dhìreadh iad na h-uain'-chnuic cho uallach ris na féidh —
Cha chuireadh teas no fuachd orra, b'e an dualchas bhith treun.

Guma fad' air ghluasad iad an eilean uain' na h-òig'
A-muigh air feadh nam buailtean 's a' cuartachadh mun chrò;
Tha pailteas dhen bhiadh ac' ann 's iad riaraichte gu leòr
'S bidh freastal a' cur dìon orra bho shìontan no ghaoth reòdht'.

Her dark heavy curly hair
Is beautiful in hue and appearance:
We got on really well,
She brought happiness to my hearth.

Our conversation was very interesting:
We talked about many places,
From the mountains of Kintail
To the cairn on Ben Bhraggie.

When she went away I was sorry,
I am always missing her:
Her image to me is as beautiful
As the flowers on the machair.

My blessings always go
To the place where she is staying —
I wish her sound sleep
And a bright happy awakening.

(*author's translation*)

The Eriskay Ponies

They've always been in Eriskay and were useful to the people,
They've been there through the centuries in times now long gone by;
They would drag home the peats with which to banish cold
And young folk would handle them and they'd give lots of fun.

To bring seaweed from the shore they were strong and plucky too,
With no trouble at all they'd bring up a pair of creels;
They would climb up the pale green hills as nimbly as the deer —
Heat and cold never bothered them, to be brave was in their blood.

May they long be on the move in the pale green isle of youth
Out amongst the sheepfolds and encircling the enclosure;
There's plenty of their food there and they're perfectly content
And providence will shelter them from storms or freezing wind.

Éiseabhal

A' dìreadh suas ri Éiseabhal gum falbh gach éislean bhuam
Is tillidh gach caomh-ghàirdeachas o m' òige dh'fhàs rium suas;
Seargaidh mulad 's crìonaidh e a-mach o chrìoch mo smuain —
Toil-inntinn nì dhomh ùrachadh air feadh do stùc is bhruach.

Gad fhaicinn anns an tràth-mhadainn, gur h-àlainn do chuid stùc,
Na h-eòin a' seinn gu bàlanta le tàlant na cruit-chiùil;
Na blianagan as bòidhche air an còmhdach leis gach flùr —
Am brù-chorcan 's am buaghallan 's am bualan ort mar chrùn.

Gum faic sinn eunlaith shònraichte am measg do chòisir-chiùil:
Tha 'n uiseag is an smeòrach ann, tha lon-dubh seinn le sunnd;
Tha crìonag-bhuidhe bhàidheil ann is fiamh as àill' bho gnùis,
Tha curracag bhreac nan sléibhtean ann is éigh aic' os do chionn.

Bidh greadanaich san òg-mhadainn gu tric aig eòin nan speur,
Bidh grinneachadh is ceòl aca nuair sheòlas iad air sgéith;
Bidh grunndachadh san fhonn aca air feadh gach tom is geug
Gu meiltreach air a loinnreachadh le loinneas a chuid fhéin.

Gur pailt a gheibhear lòghmhaireachd 'nad bhòidhchead is 'nad shnuadh,
Fàsaidh fraoch Chlann Dòmhnaill air do chòmhnardan mun cuairt;
Tha 'n t-sòbhrag bhuidhe shìobhalta gu bràth nach dìobair snuadh
A' fàs is dreach an òir oirre am measg do chòs is chluan.

Chì mi bhuam Loch Cheàrsanais a' deàrrsadh anns a' ghréin,
Glaic Ruairidh agus Màrabhal 's na torran àlainn réidh
Gu glaiceach, feurach, flùranach a' tairgsinn cliù nach géill —
Gach aon dhiubh toirt dhomh fùiteachadh do chliù a chur air ghleus.

Nach iomadh naidheachd mhìn-bheulach a dh'innseadh tu gun bhréig
Nam b' urrainn dhuit am mìneachadh gu sìobhalt' ann an sgeul;
Ach chruthaich Dia 'nad bhalbhan thu, 'nad ùrlainn bhalbh gun bheul —
Mar sin cha d'inn's thu tuairisgeal air neach a ghluais fon ghréin.

Easaval

When ascending Easaval all depression leaves me
And all the sweet joy I took from my youth comes back;
Sadness withers and fades from the edge of my thoughts —
Peace of mind refreshes me thoughout your peaks and slopes.

Seeing you early in the morning, lovely are your summits,
The birds singing lustily with all the talent of the harp;
The loveliest green patches covered with each flower —
You've the heath-rush and ragwort and groundsel as your crown.

We'll see particular birds among your musical choir:
The lark and the thrush are there, a blackbird merrily sings;
An affectionate gold-crested wren is there with the loveliest colour on her face,
The speckled lapwing of the hills is there calling out above you.

There's often early morning babble from the birds of the skies,
Making gracenotes and melody as they glide upon the wing;
They have places to land throughout each hillock and branch
Which are gently lit up by a luminescence of their own.

Splendour's found in plenty in your beauty and your hue,
The heather of Clan Donald grows on the plains around you;
The delicate yellow primrose whose colour never fades
Grows in golden magnificence amongst your nooks and lawns.

I see afar Loch Kearsinish shining in the sun,
Glaic Ruairidh and Maraval and the lovely gentle hillocks
Full of hollows, grass, and flowers and of unrivalled reputation —
Every one of them coaxing me to sing about your fame.

How many polished anecdotes could you tell without a lie
If you could only relate them calmly in a tale;
But God made you without speech, a dumb mouthless figurehead —
So you've never told a story of anyone who's ever moved.

Eilean Uibhist

Gur moch rinn mi dùsgadh san ùr-mhadainn cheòthair,
Bheir ceilearadh nan smeòrach dhomh ceòlraidh as ùr:
Bidh fonn air gach creutair ag éirigh le sòlas
An eilean gorm an eòrn' thug dhomh beòthadh bho thùs;
Uibhist ghorm nan stùcan 's nam machraichean flùrach,
Nam beanntanan rùnach air an crùnadh le fraoch,
Tìr àraich a' chluarain bhios gu bràth dhuinn 'na shuaithneas —
Gach àit' anns an gluais sinn bidh e fuaight' ruinn le gaol.

An t-eilean uain' bàidheil 's e cuartaicht' le sàile,
Bidh nuallan an làin anns na bàigh air gach taobh:
Tha 'n Cuan an-Iar mun cuairt air le gairge an uabhais,
Toirt bàirlinn tha cruaidh dhuinn nuair ghluaiseas a' ghaoth;
Toirt beairteas gu 'chòrsa, toirt feamainn do na cròicean,
Toirt pailteas de bheòshlaint is stòras is maoin —
Tha eunlaith a' tàmh ann, tha biadh do'n cuid àil ann,
Tha 'n t-seamrag as àille a' fàs air na raoin.

Gur h-inntinneach gluasad a-mach feadh nam buailtean,
A' coiseachd feadh na luachrach 's dol cuairt feadh an fhraoich,
A' dìreadh nan stùcan bheir inntinn is sunnd dhomh
'S gun dìobair gach cùram th' air cùlaibh mo smaoin;
Toirt beachd air gach àilleachd a th' air maise nàdair
A chruthaicheadh on àirde le làmh Rìgh nan Dùl —
Tha pailteas gach seòrsa an Uibhist ghorm an eòrna
A' fuadachadh bròin bhuam 'nam òige 's 'nam aois.

Gur taitneach le m' inntinn m'a bhòidhchead bhith sgrìobhadh:
Tha dhealbh dhomh cho rìomhach 's a chìtear le sùil,
Ged s fhad' on bha d' àilleachd air fhilleadh am bàrdachd
Aig seanchaidhean 's luchd dhàn a tha cnàmh anns an ùir;
Am beagan th' air fhàgail a' leughadh maise nàdair
'S a dh'fhiosraich mar thà e 's mar bhà e o thùs,
Gur toil leinn bhith 'g innse mu eilean ar sinnsear
'Na laighe sa Chuan Sgìth 's do na linntean cha d' mhùth.

Cutting reeds for annual thatching, September 1999 (Photograph by Paul Haley)

New thatch was laid over the old, held down with chicken wire, then treated with weedkiller (Photograph by Paul Haley)

The reeds were stooked until partly dried (Photograph by Paul Haley)

Donald MacDonald, self-sufficient in his kitchen (Photograph by Dòmhnall Iain Caimbeul)

The Isle of Uist

It's early I awoke in the misty young morning,
For the warbling of the thrushes brings me music afresh:
All creatures hum with joy as they rise with gladness
In the blue-green isle of barley that gave me life from the start;
Blue-green Uist of the peaks and of the flower-covered machairlands,
The beloved mountains that are crowned with heather,
The land that nurtured the thistle that will always be our symbol —
Every place in which we walk is made a part of us by love.

The loving green island that's surrounded by brine,
The roar of the tide fills the bays on each side:
The Atlantic surrounds it with its appalling ferocity,
Giving us harsh warning when the wind begins to move;
Bringing wealth to its coast, and seaweed to the rocks,
Bringing plenty of livelihood and money and wealth —
Birds make their nests there, there's food for their brood there,
And the loveliest clover grows on the fields.

It's inspiring to walk out amongst the enclosures,
Strolling through rushes and walking through heather,
Climbing the summits that cheer and inspire me
Till all worries are banished from the back of my mind;
Viewing each kind of beauty that nature possesses
Made from above by the King of the Elements —
Blue-green Uist of barley has enough of each species
To dispel all my sadness in youth and old age.

It pleases my mind to write of its loveliness:
To me its picture's as pretty as can be seen with the eye,
Though it's long since your charms were turned into poetry
By shennachies and poets who rot in the soil;
For the few who're left reading of natural beauty
And have known how things are and were from the start,
We love to be telling of our ancestors' island
Which lies in the Minch in defiance of change.

Nuair thig an cadal buan 's nach cuir mi feum air cluasaig
'S a chàirear leis an t-sluagh mi san fhuar-leabaidh dhùint',
A' ghainmheach bhith mun cuairt dhomh 's am muran gorm mu m' uachdar
'S an duslach anns 'n do ghluais mi gam chuartach' as ùr,
Mhiannaichinn bhith 'n càradh measg eòlach agus chàirdean
('S gur pailt iad ann a Hàllann a' cnàmh anns an ùir)
Ann an eilean gorm mo shinnsear, mun d'rinn mi seo a sgrìobhadh
A théid a sheinn gu cinnteach le binn-bheul a' chiùil.

Éiseabhal Stùcach

Éiseabhal stùcach nan ùr-bhlàth 's nan cluan
'S nan aibhnichean siùbhlach 's an cùrsa gu cuan,
Nan gorm-ghlaicean flùrach tha ùrail 'nan snuadh —
'S tha 'n t-sòbhrag 's an cluaran a' fàs ann.

Bho s dual dha mo nàdar bhith tàthadh nan duan
'S a' sgrìobhadh na Gàidhlig gun àrdan gun uaill,
Gun sgaoil mi mo thàlant an-dràst' ort mun cuairt
'S gun inn's mi don t-sluagh mu d' chuid bhòidhchid.

Glinn air an còmhdach le còinneach 's le fraoch,
An t-sòbhrag 's an neòinean ag òradh nan raon,
A' chaora le h-òg-uain faighinn lòn air gach taobh
'S an smeòrach gu saor ri cuid ceòlraidh.

Sléibhtean bheir sòlas is sòighneas don t-sùil
Ri'm faicinn 'nan glòir anns an òg-mhadainn chiùin;
Nuair sgaoileas an ceò gheibh sinn eòlas as ùr
Air àilleachd gach flùir feadh na mòintich.

Mu bhruaichean do chaochain tha caoin-bhiolair uain',
Tha lìon nam ban sìth ann as rìomhaiche snuadh;
Tha sealbhag nam fiadh ann, 's an fhìor bharrag ruadh,
'S tha roid mar as dualach a' fàs ann.

When it's time to sleep forever with no need for a pillow
And I'm placed by the people in the cold enclosed bed,
With sand all around me and blue-green bents above me
And the dust in which I came to life surrounding me once more,
I'd wish to be deposited with friends and relations
(And they're plentiful in Hallin decaying in the soil)
In my forebears' blue-green island, the subject of my writing
Which will certainly be sung by the sweet mouth of music.

Craggy Easaval

Craggy Easaval of fresh blossoms and lawns
And fast-flowing rivers whose course is to the sea,
Of rich green flower-filled hollows which are fresh and bright in colour —
And the primrose and thistle are growing there.

Since it's in my very blood to be composing poems
And writing in Gaelic with no excess of pride,
I'll spread all my talents around you just now
And I'll inform the people of your beauty.

Glens that are covered in moss and in heather,
The primrose and daisy gilding the lawns,
The ewe with her young lambs are grazing on each side
And the thrush is making music in freedom.

Hills that give pleasure and joy to the eye
When seen in their glory in the young morning's calm;
When the mist lifts its curtain we'll renew our acquaintance
With the beauty of each flower in the moorland.

Round the banks of your streamlet is gentle green watercress,
Fairy flax is there with the loveliest hue;
Mountain sorrel is there, and the real yellow-horned poppy,
And bog-myrtle grows there as usual.

Nuair dheàrrsas a' ghrian ort gur ciatach do ghnùis:
Gach glaic agus blianag cho fìor-ghlan fo dhriùchd,
Do chnuic is do réidhlein 'nan éideadh gun smùr —
'S tha fiamh far do chrùin mar an t-òmar.

Ged shéideadh an dùdlachd gu h-ùdlaidh bhon iar
Sa gheamhradh le buaireas a' ruagadh nan sìon,
Bidh sìochaint is sàmhchair 'nad fhàs-sgorran ciar'
A' tàladh na h-eunlaith tha beò annt'.

Bidh 'n sneachd' anns an fhaoilteach ag aomadh mu d' bhàrr,
Bidh 'n t-sòbhrag mu d' alltain am Bealltainn na Màigh' —
Bidh cuairtean na bliadhna gad riaghladh gu bràth
Ged as crìon anns an làr do luchd-eòlais.

Tìr nan Raon

Tìr nan raon 's nan glaicean uain',
Tìr nam bruach 's nam bealach
Far 'm bi na tuinn a' tighinn gu tràigh
'S far 'n dèan na crà-gheòidh fantainn.

A dh'ainneoin sneachda 's gaillinn fuair
Tha geamhradh gruamach seachad
'S tha earrach, ùrachd sunnd na h-òig',
Air tighinn le deòin gu'r cladach.

Nuair thig a' Bhealltainn oirnn mun cuairt
Bidh guth na cuaich' sna gleannan
A' tighinn air sgéith á tìrean céin'
'S gun dèan i sgeul dhuinn aithris.

Bheir toit an fhraoich air ais ar n-òig'
Is iomadh spòrs bha tlachdmhor,
A' dèanamh falaisg feadh nam beann,
A' fuadach greann is airtneal.

When the sun shines upon you your expression is lovely:
Every hollow and greensward so pure under dew,
Your hillocks and plains in their unblemished raiment —
  And your crown has a sheen like amber.

Should the breeze of the doldrums growl from the west
In winter with ferment expelling the storms,
The silence and peace in your lonely grey summits
  Send the birds who nest there to sleep.

The snow in the wolftime will curl round your summit,
The primrose round your burns in the Beltane of May —
The annual cycles will rule you forever
  Though your friends lie decayed in the ground.

The Land of the Fields

Land of the fields and the pale-green hollows,
  Land of the passes and braes
Where the waves roll in upon the beaches
  And the shelduck fly in to stay.

In spite of the snow and the chilly storm
  Surly winter has now gone by
And spring, renewal of youthful joy,
  Has come willingly to our shore.

When Beltane comes around to us
  The cuckoo's heard in the valleys
As she comes on the wing from distant lands
  In order to tell us her story.

The smoke of the heather brings back our youth
  With its many pleasant diversions,
Making the muirburn around the hills,
  Expelling glooms and depressions.

Nuair a thig an t-Sultuin àigh
    Gur àlainn bhios na seallaidh,
Bidh fraoch nam beann 'na uile ghlòir
    Le iomadh seòrsa dhathan.

Bidh uaine 's purpur 'm measg a-chéil',
    A' seudachadh 'nam maise
Mar bhogha-frois sa mhadainn thràth
    A thig tro sgàil nam frasan.

Bidh smeòrach ghlas air cnuic a' seinn,
    Tha aoibhneas 'na cuid caithreim;
Bidh seillean srianach triall le srann
    Bho fhlùr gu plannd 'na dheannaibh.

Bidh fear na speal' air achadh buain,
    Is sruth bho ghruaidh de dh'fhallas,
Bidh ceangladair gu trang 'na dhéidh
    Cur sguab gu réidh sna bannan.

Bidh fear le sùist a' froiseadh dhias
    'S an sìol gun téid a' bharraich;
Is ás a-sin chun an damh-sùirn
    'S bhon t-sùirn chun an àth-bhracha.

Ma thig an t-saothair thoirt gu crìoch
    Bidh iomadh nì ri tachairt —
Bidh am muileann is a' bhrà
    Gu làidir cur nan car dhiubh.

Nuair théid a h-uile rud air dòigh
    Bidh iomadh seòrs' am pailteas —
Biadh is aran air a' bhòrd
    Is deur de stòr na bracha.

When glorious September comes
    There are beautiful sights to see,
Mountain heather in all its glory
    With many kinds of colours.

Pale green and purple intermingle,
    Glistening in their beauty
Like an early morning rainbow
    Emerging from a veil of showers.

A grey thrush sings upon the hills,
    There's joy in her exulting;
A striped bee travels with a buzz
    From flower to plant in hurriedness.

The scyther's on the harvest field,
    Sweat streaming down his cheek,
The binder's busy in his wake
    Neatly tying up the sheaves.

A man beats ears of corn with a flail
    Till the crop has turned into seed;
From there it goes to the oven joist
    And from the oven to the malt-kiln.

If the work's brought to an end
    Many things must happen —
The mill and the quern
    Will be strongly turning.

When everything's in order
    There'll be many kinds of plenty —
Food and bread upon the table
    And a drop of malted produce.

Mìosan na Bliadhna

AM FAOILTEACH

Storim is gailleann 's deilge shìontan,
Frasan sneachda 's càblaid fhiadhaich,
Reodh-ghaoth snaidheadh feadh nan crìochan,
Aimsir ùdlaidh;
Aingealtachd air fiamh nan speuran,
Splèachdach neòil air aodann gréine,
Connspaid iargailleach ag éirigh
Air na dùilean;
Mìos an fhaoiltich rinn a dhranndail,
Toirt gu chrìch an ràidhe geamhraidh,
Géilleachdainn do thìm 'na deann-ruith
Triall a chùrsa.

AN GEARRAN

Aiteamh agus tuiltean dìle
Dòrtadh oirnn a-nuas gun dìobradh,
Aibhnichean a' ruith 'nan still
Gu iomadh sàile;
Monmhair fhann aig tuinn nan cuantan
Sluaisreadh ris na creagan cruaidh-chas
Far 'n do shaothraich iad gun bhuannachd
Troimh na linntean;
Truaghantachd a' lorg gach creutair,
Deò na beath' air thuar an tréigsinn —
Teachd-an-tìr cho gann dha'm feuman
Anns an sguabaig.

AM MÀRT

Mìos an-iochdar, greannach, ascaoin,
Trògbhoil gamhlais teann dha daonnan —
Tàsanachd gun truas ri daoine
No ri creutair;

The Months of the Year

JANUARY

Storm and tempest and skewer of hurricanes,
Showers of snow and angry confusion,
Icy wind carving its way through the land,
Surly weather;
Wickedness in the skies' expression,
Squinting are clouds on the face of the sun,
Warlike dispute comes up to the surface
Of the elements;
The month of the wolftime has given its snarl,
Bringing an end to the winter quarter,
Ceding to time in her frantic onrush
Its momentum.

FEBRUARY

Along with thaw comes rain in torrents
Pouring down on us unceasing,
Rivers run in waterspouts
To many sea-lochs;
The distant roar of ocean waves
Lashing on the rocky cliffs
Where they've toiled without avail
Down through the ages;
Wretchedness seeks out each creature,
The vital spark has all but left them —
Their food's inadequate for their needs
In the sweeper.

MARCH

Month that's surly, merciless, and harsh,
Malicious grumbling never far from it —
Fretting with no sympathy to men
Or to creature;

Miadhalachd na sàmhchair sìochaint
Cha robh fasgadh dhaibh m'a chrìochan
'Na chuid sheòmar;
Séideadh balg le garbhachd tuasaid
Cur an céill nan euchdan truaillidh
Dearbhadh g'eil an claidheamh cruadhach
Teann 'na chrògan,
Toirt am follais dhuinn le daors'
Gur mìos a' Mhàirt e.

A' GHIBLIN

Caochladh tìde 's sìneadh soillse,
Soinneantachd is sìth an aoibhnis,
Tilgeadh òglaidheachd neo-choibhneil
Tharna uthard;
Monmhair bhinn aig uillt nam beanntan
Ruith gu réidh troimh àilean greannmhor
Caisleadh morghain agus gainmheach
Thar nam mulan;
A' churracag bhreac thug bàrr le bòidhche
Air gach eun thug plaosg gu beothaich
No gu eirte
Neadachadh air feadh an fheòir
'S tighinn beò le dìcheall.

AM MÀIGH

Mìos an aoibhnis is an oirchis
Air bheil ainm na maighdinn shònraichte
Air bheil bunaitean mo dhòchais
Air an stéidheadh;
Ionaltradh aig buar is caoirich
Criomadh feòir measg bhòidhche raointean
Agus réidhlean;
Laoigh is uain a' falbh 'nan deann-ruith
A' cluich cho saor am braon an t-samhraidh,
A' bhanachag le ceuman uallach
Dol a bhleoghainn a' chruidh ghuaillfhinn
Chun na h-àirigh.

Respectability of peace and quiet
Found no shelter round its bounds
In its chambers;
Bellows blowing with violent tumult
Representing the corrupted deeds
To prove it holds the sword of steel
Tight in its fists,
Making it clear to us with dearth
That it is March.

APRIL

Change of weather and longer light,
Mildness and the peace of joy,
Casting unkind ugliness
Away on high;
Mountain streams' melodious murmuring
Running gently through lovely meadow
Stirring up the sand and gravel
Over shingle;
The speckled lapwing who beats for beauty
Any bird that has brought shell to life
Or to fulfilment
Builds her nest amongst the grass
And works hard to live.

MAY

Month of happiness and kindness
That bears the special virgin's name
On which my optimism's foundations
Are established;
Grazing for cattle and for sheep
Which nibble grass amongst the beauties
Of fields and plains;
Calves and lambs are dashing madly
Playing so free in summer's dew,
The milkmaid with her haughty steps
Going to milk white-shouldered cattle
On the shieling.

AN T-ÒGMHIOS

Grian na glòir-réim anns na speuran,
Dòrtadh oirnn a blàths gu'r feuman —
Ìocshlaint do a h-uile creutair
A tha gluasad;
Speachantachd air tighinn san eunlaith
Cumail nàimhdean far a crìochan
Gus an àl a thoirt gu tèarainte
Gu eirte;
Clann ag atharrais guth na cuaiche
Le cruit-chiùil air feadh nam bruachan
Toirt a ceòlraidh nall thar chuan
Gu treòrach inntinn;
Seillean ruadh a' saothair sunndach
Deoghal mil á uchd nam flùran —
Bruailleanachd a' dol air dìochuimhn'
Ann am blàths an Ògmhios chiataich
Thug dhuinn sùgradh.

AN T-IUCHAR

Feur gu àilgheas cruidh is chaorach
Fàs air achaidhean is caolshrath,
Am buachaille gun uaill no gaoid
Ag iomain tàine;
Gucag-bhàitht' nam bileag uaine
Fàs am measg na cuilc cho snuadhmhor —
Sann le dànadas a bhuainear
I bho frìth-bhac;
Uiseagan gu h-àrd sna speuran
Le'n cuid luinneagan gan gleusadh,
Meadhrachais am measg a-chéile
Cho sgèimh uallach;
Toradh buaile pailt ri fhaotainn,
Cuachan làn de bhainne daonnan
Gu ar càileachd;
Maise nàdair loinneil fhlùrach
Air a measgadh ann an ùr-fhàs
A' cur sealladh thar na dùthcha

JUNE

The sun rules gloriously in the skies,
Pouring her warmth on us for our needs —
Medicine for every creature
That is moving;
Waspishness in birds' behaviour
Keeping enemies off their bounds
So that they can safely bring
Their brood to strength;
Children mimic the voice of the cuckoo
Who with her lyre around the braes
Has brought her music across the sea
To inspire the mind;
Yellow bumble-bee cheerfully toiling
To suck the honey from bosoms of flowers —
Melancholy thoughts are being forgotten
In the warmth of beautiful June
That's given us joy.

JULY

Grass to the taste of cows and sheep
Growing upon fields and narrow strath,
The herdboy unspoilt and unblemished
Driving cattle;
The water-lily with its pale green leaves
Growing amongst the elegant reeds —
It takes audacity to pluck
Her from her barb;
Larks on high up in the skies
Busy practising their ditties,
Frolicking amongst each other
So fair and proud;
Yield of cowfold in abundance,
Cups at all times full of milk
To satisfy us;
Nature's rampant flowering beauty
Mixed together with growth that's new
Making the countryside appear

A tha bòidheach,
Dealt a' priobadh oirnn cho caoin
Am measg nan ròsan.

AN LÙNASTAL

Abaichead a' tighinn san arbhar,
Diasan eòrn' a' fàs gu tairbhe
Fear na tuatha;
A h-uile creutair a tha gluasad
A' fàilteachadh na gartmhoir' suairce
A chaidh a bhuileachadh an lànmhoir' —
Taitneadh tiodhlaic diadhachd ghràsmhoir;
Speuran soilleir gun fiamh orr'
Saor bho pheileasaich nan sìontan,
Làithean sona, sìtheil, soirmeil
Saor bho aingealtachd is foireigneadh:
Fonn is aoibhneas feadh nan cluaintean,
Sunnd is gean 'nar leum 's 'nar gluasad.

AN T-SULTUINE

Meadhoin foghair drip na buana
Tional bàrr tha abaich cnuasmhor,
Deisealachd air son nan cruachan
Air a geàrd bho ghéire tuath-ghaoith':
Iodhlannan a' sealltainn saoibhir
Le pailteas co-roinn chruidh laoigh is ghamhnan;
Frionas bheag sa ghaoith on eara-dheas
Ag aithris caochladh tighinn san aimsir —
Neòil a' falach bhuainn na reultan,
Gealach sealgair anns na speuran
Dearbhadh gu bheil spòrs taigh-céilidh
Teannadh dlùth dhuinn.

AN DÀMHAIR

Seargadh a' tighinn anns na blàthan,
Gach lus is flùr a' call an àilleachd,
An dath purpaidh bòidheach greannmhor

Quite beautiful,
With dew that gently winks at us
Amongst the roses.

August

Ripeness comes upon the oats,
While ears of barley grow to meet
The landsman's needs;
Every creature that's astir
Welcomes the kind munificence
That's been liberally bestowed —
The pleasure of the gift of a gracious deity;
Clear skies without a trace of gloom
Free from the pestering of storms,
Happy, peaceful, harmonious days
Free from wickedness and violence:
Delight and cheer throughout the fields,
Content and joy in our spring and our walk.

September

Haste of reaping in mid-autumn
Gathering crop that's ripe and fruitful,
The preparations for the cornstacks
Guarded from the north wind's sting:
Cornyards looking well-endowed
With plenty to share for milk cows and stirks;
A little snarl in the south-east wind
Reveals a change to come in the weather —
The stars concealed from us by clouds,
While in the skies the hunter's moon
Proves that ceilidh-house entertainment
Is coming near us.

October

Withering comes upon the blooms,
Each herb and flower is drained of beauty,
The neat and lovely purple hue

A dh'fhàg cho loinneil fraoch nam beanntan
A-nis a' call a dhreach bha snuadhmhor
Ann an osag na gaoith' tuatha;
Cuid dhen aimsir ciatach tìorail
'S cuid dhith coirbt' a' maoidheadh dìoghail —
Feasgar foghair triall 'na ghluasad
Mar ruidhleadh clach ri beinn nan uain'-ghleann.

AN T-SAMHAIN

Srann clach-mheallain tighinn bhon iarmailt',
Sneachda 's clàmhainn 's aimsir fhiadhaich,
Buirbeachd na gaoith' an iar-thuath
Séideadh làidir;
Tuinn na mara teachd gu còrsa
A' dol 'nan still air feadh nan cròicean;
Sad na fairge sealltainn strìtheil
'S air am bàrran marcachd-shìne,
An cuan air a mhaistreadh measg a-chéile —
'S a dh'ainneoin a' bhirlinn a bhith làidir
Tha crann-siùil a' lùbadh ri ùmhlachd sàraich'.

AN DÙBHLACHD

A dh'ainneoin dranndail 's fead na docair
Tighinn bhon eara-dheas coirbte dòbhaidh,
Tha Dùbhlachd ùdlaidh a' toirt àbhachd
Is sunnd is gean air gnùis nam pàistean,
An cridheachan air mhir le sòlas
A' feitheamh bodach mór na còiread
A' tighinn troimhn t-similear gu falachaidh —
'S air a h-aon cha dèan e dearmad;
Sluagh a' cruinneachadh ann an càirdeas
A' toirt moladh dhan Dia as àirde
A thug maitheanas is saorsainn
Is sìth is sèimhe do shluagh an t-saoghail.

That left the heather of the hills so pretty
Now loses its colourful appearance
In the gust of the northerly breeze;
Some of the weather is lovely and dry
And some of it perversely threatens vengeance —
The autumn evening goes in its momentum
As a stone would roll down a hill of green glens.

NOVEMBER

A rattle of hailstones comes from the sky,
Snow and sleet and boisterous weather,
The wildness of a north-westerly wind
Blowing strongly;
The waves of the ocean come in to the shore
Whipped into spouts around weed-covered rocks;
The breaking wavetops appear aggressive
With spindrift running along their tips,
The sea's being churned and is all in confusion —
And despite the birlinn being sturdily built
Her mast bows humbly to the oppressor.

DECEMBER

For all the troublesome growling and whistling
Coming from the south-east vicious and unruly,
Gloomy December brings with it merriment
And happiness and cheer to children's faces,
Their hearts going into spasms of delight
As they wait for the big old man of kindness
Coming secretly through the chimney —
And never a child will he ever forget;
People gather together in friendship
Giving praise to God in the highest
Who brought forgiveness and redemption
And peace and serenity to all mankind.

Mo Reul Iùil

Dheàrrsaich solas aoibhnis dhomh,
'S b'e soillse mo reul iùil:
Mar shoilleireachd nan coinnlean
A' boillsgeadh air na bùird;
Shiab air falbh an duibhre
'S chaidh brat na h-oidhch' air chùl
'S bha cuireadh cùirteil blàth-chridheach
Gam fhàilteachadh as ùr.

Dh'fhalbh na sgòthan aognaidh ud
Is thàinig gaol 'nan àit',
Dh'éirich grian na h-aoighealachd
Is caoine na mìos Màigh;
Bha madainn bhlàth na caomhalachd
A' sgaoileadh gathan tlàiths
'S bha ceileireachd is ceòlraidh
A' cur beòthalachd 'nam phàirt.

Mar ghaoth thar bhàrr nam flùran
Fo dhriùchd na madainn chéit':
Tha t' anail bhlàth 'na cùbhraidheachd
Mar ùbhlan air a' gheug;
Tha t' ìomhaigh chàirdeil ùrlaimh
Mar chrùn fo mhùirneachd sheud —
'S mar shneachd' air iomall stùcan
Tha ùrarachd do dheud.

Tha cuailean dualach rìomhach ort
Mar dhìtheanan an òir
A' dol 'na stuadhan dì-snaidhm
'S a' chìr ga cur an dlòth;
Ga phleatadh ann an snuadhachadh
'S ga shuaineadh anns a' chòrn —
'S gur bòidheach mu do ghualainn e,
Cur loinn is uaisl' 'nad chòir.

My Guiding Star

A gleam of pleasure shone for me,
    It was my guiding star's light:
Like the brightness of the candles
    Flickering on tables;
The darkness cleared away
    And the cloak of night fell back
And a kind warm-hearted greeting
    Welcomed me again.

Those terrifying clouds have gone
    And love's come in their place,
Hospitality's sun has risen
    And the gentleness of May;
The warm morning of kindness
    Have spread their mellow rays
And the birdsong and the music
    Have brought me back to life.

Like the breeze across the flowers
    Under maytime morning dew:
Your warm breath in its fragrance
    Is like apples on a branch;
Your friendly neat appearance
    Is like a crown of dainty jewels —
And like snow on flanks of hilltops
    Is the freshness of your teeth.

You have glorious curling hair
    Resembling golden flowers
Soaring in smooth billows
    Locked fast with a comb;
Beautifully plaited
    And twisted into a braid —
And it's lovely round your shoulders,
    Lending elegance and charm.

Gur bòidhche leam do ghluasad
Na raointean uain' fo bhlàth
Nuair as àille bhios na cluaintean
Le neòinean snuadhmhor bàn;
Tha teòchridheachd fuaighte riut,
'S tu le fuil na h-uaisle làn,
Tha 'n sunnd a tha gad chuartachadh
Mar cheòl na cuaich' sa Mhàigh.

Tha do phearsa 'na bheusalachd
Mar éirigh gréin' air stùc
Air madainn bhòidheach chéiteineach
'S an dealt cur geis feadh fhlùr;
Tha do chòmhradh réidh-labhairt
Mar ghleusadh teud a' chiùil
Gu togail suas ar n-inntinnean
Is mì-ghean chur air chùl.

Gur eireachdail' air ùrlar thu
Na gàrradh-fhlùr fo bhlàth,
Cho dreachmhor ris an ùrchoill'
Fo ungadh driùchd bho 'n àird;
Mar bhogha-frois' san iarmailt
Le dathan ciatach àigh
'S gach ceann dheth ann am fìon-lios
Gu riarachadh ar càil.

S binne leam do chòmhradh
Na roghainn còisir chiùil,
No fann-ghaoth madainn Chéitein
Le séideag réiteachd rùin;
Tha thu mar fhuaran fìor-ghlan
Tha pailt gu ìotas bùirn
A shil bho bhàrr na h-iarmailt
Gu ìoc-lus anns a' ghrunnd.

Tha do mhuineal glé-gheal
Mar dhéideag air an tràigh,
Mar shneachd' air mullach Éiseabhail
An géiread a' mhìos Mhàirt;

I find more beauty in your walk
    Than in blossoming green meadows
When the fields are at their loveliest
    With gorgeous white daisies;
Warmheartedness is part of you,
    Being full of excellent blood,
And cheerfulness encircles you
    Like cuckoo's music in May.

Your character's as perfect
    As sunrise on a mountain peak
On a lovely maytime morning
    When the dew enchants the flowers;
Your smoothly-spoken discourse
    Is like the plucking of a harpstring
To lift up our minds
    And banish discontent.

You're better poised on a dance-floor
    Than a flower-garden in bloom,
As fine in form as young forest
    Anointed by heaven's dew;
Like a rainbow in the sky
    With pretty colours from providence
And each end of it in vineyards
    To gratify our tastes.

Sweeter to me is your talk
    Than the finest musical choir,
Or the breeze of a May morning
    Blowing gently to calm desire;
You're like a pure spring of water
    Abundant for quenching thirst
That has rained from the top of the sky
    To a healing-plant down in the ground.

Your neck is of perfect white
    Like a pebblestone on the beach,
Like snow on Easaval's summit
    In the bitterness of March;

Mar eala bhàn nan cuantan
Air bhàrr nan stuadh a' snàmh,
No ceò air iomall Bheinn Chruachain —
Taobh tuath de dh'Earra-Ghàidheal.

Nuair chì mi 'm measg a' chòmhlain thu
Bidh thu mar ròs fo bhlàth,
Cho aoigheil agus còmhraiteach
'S cho bòidheach ann ad' ghnàths;
Mo dhùrachd-sa an còmhnaidh dhut
Gach sòlas bhith 'nad phàirt —
'S nam faighinn mar a dh'òrdaichinn,
Gum bi thu beò gu bràch.

An Uibhist ghorm an eòrna
'Nad òige rinn thu fàs
Far 'm bi na tonnan crònanach
A' connspaid air an tràigh —
Far bheil fraoch Chlann Dòmhnaill
A' còmhdach nam beann àrd'
'S far 'n dèan an calman còmhnaidh
Mar as deòin leis, anns na càirn.

Òran Step

(Sgeama Cruthachadh Obrach)

Ged a tha mi fàs aosta
'S craiceann m' aodainn air ciaradh
'S an geamhradh greannach le dhùire
A' teannadh dlùth ri mo chrìochan,
Tha mi 'm-bliadhna cho spòrsail
Ri gille-òg ann am fìor-ghaol —
Ged bhiodh fàinneachan òir
Air mo mheòirean 'nan ceudan,
'S mi nis aig Step.

Like the white swan of the oceans
   Swimming on top of the waves,
Or mist on the side of Ben Cruachan —
   The north Coastland of the Gael.

When I see you surrounded by people
   You're like a rose in full bloom,
So hospitable and talkative
   And so beautiful in your ways;
My good wishes are yours forever
   That you may enjoy every happiness —
And if I could get what I'd ask for,
   You'll have the gift of life eternal.

In blue-green Uist of the barley
   You grew up when you were young
Where the ever-murmuring waves
   Debate upon the beach —
Where the heather of Clan Donald
   Covers the high hills
And where the dove will make its home
   As it likes to, in the rocks.

The Step Song

(Jobs Creation Scheme)

Though I'm growing old
   With the skin of my face getting paler
And surly winter with its dourness
   Coming close to my territory,
This year I'm as active
   As a love-torn adolescent —
As if I had gold rings
   On my fingers in hundreds,
                  Being now with Step.

Ged tha mi fo mhùigeachd
  A-muigh air chùlaibh na mòintich
Gun daoine tighinn dlùth dhomh
  A nì rium sùgradh no còmhradh,
Tha eunlaith nan speuran
  Air an éideadh cho bòidheach
'S iad gach là rium ag éigheach:
  "Siud thu, eudail a Dhòmhnaill —
        Tha thu aig Step."

Thig an t-airgead dhomh feumail:
  Gheibh mi léin' agus còta,
Théid mi 'nam éideadh
  Mar na reultan le leòmachd;
Gheibh mi botal deoch làidir
  A nì slànach' dha m' dhòchas
'S a chuireas sradag 'nam thàlann
  Air chor 's gun càin mi gu'm brògan
        Muinntir Step.

Cha b'e càineadh a dh'fheumainn:
  Tha iad reusanta 's uasal,
Thug iad furtachd dha m' éiginn
  Nuair nach dèanainn feum anns a' chruaidh-ghleac;
Nuair thig MacAsgaill Di-Haoine
  Tillidh aoibh, 's teichidh gruaman —
Sann a dh'fhàsas mi aotrom
  A-muigh air aodann nan cruadhlach
        Aig obair Step.

Sann a thilleas an òige
  Agus dòighealachd ùr thugam,
'S théid mi cuairt sìos gu m' eòlas
  Mu chòrs Àird nan Srùban;
Nuair théid a' cheist a chur dòigheil
  Bidh freagairt shònraicht' gam ionnsaigh
'S nì mi Raonaid a phòsadh —
  Ged bhiodh m' òg-bhean fo dhiombadh
        Aig muinntir Step.

Though I get moody
  Out at the back of the hill
With no-one coming near me
  For diversion or converse,
The birds of the skies
  Are so beautifully clad
As they cry to me daily:
  "Oh it's you, Donald darling —
        And you're with Step."

The money will be useful:
  I'll get a shirt and a coat,
And when I dress up
  I'll be posh like the filmstars;
I'll get a bottle of hard stuff
  To salvage my hopes
And put a spark to my talents
  For tearing strips off those Step folk
        Down to their shoes.

Not that I should complain:
  They're reasonable and polite,
They helped me out in my crisis
  When the struggle defeated me;
When MacAskill comes on Friday
  Cheer will return, gloom will flee —
Indeed I'll grow quite light-hearted
  Out there on the rockface
        Working for Step.

My youth will come back
  With new expectations,
And down I'll go to my friends
  Round the Àird nan Srùban shore;
When the question's put properly
  I'll get a positive reply
And I'll marry Rachel —
  Though my bride might annoy
        The folk from Step.

Nì sinn dachaigh an Rònaigh
  Far 'n gin eòrna 's buntàta:
Bidh iasg dhe gach seòrsa
  A' snàmh mu chòrsa nam bàgh ann;
Ged a shéideadh an tuath-ghaoth
  Gheibh sinn uamha bhios sàbhailt' —
Fads bhios m' òg-bhean ri m' ghualainn
  Cha bhi gruaimean gu bràch orm
    'S mi aig Step.

FREAGAIRT RAONAID

Cha b'e seann daoine riaslach
  Bu mhiann leam air chluasaig
Ach òganach ciatach
  A chumadh rian air mo bhuaidhean,
'S a thigeadh dhachaigh Di-Haoine
  An déidh a shaothair a bhuannachd
'S a chuireadh ceud not air a' bhòrd dhomh —
  'S chan e ròcais na truaighe
    A tha aig Step!

Tha sgall ort gu d' chùlaibh
  'S chan eil thu flùrach bho d' bhialaibh,
Tha dearbhadh 'nad ghnùis
  Nach d' chuir thu ùidh anns an t-siabann;
'S mas e cùl Eilein Rònaigh
  Àite còmhnaidh do mhiann-sa,
Se mo ghuidhe 's mo dhòchas
  Gun dèan na ròin ann do stialladh
    'S mar sin leat.

AN CO-DHÙNADH

Fàsaidh feur air na raointean,
  Fàsaidh fraoch air a' mhòintich,
Tillidh Bealltainn is faoilteach
  Gu Uibhist ghaolach Chlann Dhòmhnaill,

We'll make a home in Ronay
   Where potatoes and barley take:
All sorts of fish will be swimming
   Round the shores of the bays there;
Though the north wind may blow
   We'll find a cave that's secure —
While my bride's at my shoulder
   I'll never be gloomy
            Since I'm with Step.

RACHEL'S ANSWER

It's not an old man who's troublesome
   That I'd like on my pillow
But a young man who's wholesome
   And a match for my virtues,
Who'd come home on Fridays
   Well paid for his labour
And put a hundred pounds on the table —
   Not that miserable pittance
            You get from Step!

From behind you're a baldie
   And from the front you're no flower,
There is proof in your face
   That in soap you've no interest;
And if the back end of Ronay
   Is the home of your dreams,
I just pray and hope
   The seals have you for breakfast there
            And so bye bye.

THE CONCLUSION

Grass will grow on the fields
   And heather on moorland,
May and wolftime will return
   To darling Uist of Clan Donald,

Bidh lìonadh is tràghadh
Mar as gnàth anns na h-òban
Agus sinne ann an sàmhchair,
Air ar càramh fo fhòidean
'S gun chuimhn' air Step.

Triall na h-Ùine

Nuair thriallas bhuainn na bliadhnaichean
Thig iargain oirnn is gruaim,
Bidh imcheist air ar n-inntinnean
Is iomachruth air ar snuadh;
Bidh dòigh is beachdan ùr' againn,
'S ar cùrs' air tighinn mun cuairt
Na rubhaichean thug riasladh dhuinn
'S chum sìos sinn air ar cuairt.

Cha tàinig e don t-saoghal seo
'S cha tig a h-aon gu bràth —
Cho goirid 's gum bi 'n ùin' aige
Ma chì a shùil an là —
Nach fiosraich trioblaid thalmhaidheach
Measg soirbheachaidh is bàidh,
Cho aithghearr 's gum bi chuairt againn
Tha duais dhuinn anns a' bhàs.

Ma gheibh sinn àireamh bhliadhnaichean
Mun iarrar sinn a-null,
Bidh iomaluaisg agus deacaireachd
Is dearmail tighinn dhuinn dlùth;
Bidh meirg a' tighinn le màirnealachd
'S théid mànranachd air chùl —
Ar n-inntinn fàsaidh riaghailteach,
Is riaspach gun chus sunnd.

Air ais gur tric a' sealltainn sinn
Mun gheall a fhuair sinn òg
(A chosg ar n-ùin' a' geòbraich)
Gun gheamhradh ri tighinn òirnn:

Tides high and low
Will flow through inlets as usual
As we lie in silence,
Placed under the sods
Without memory of Step.

The Passage of Time

When the years start escaping us
We grow worried and morose,
Anxiety preys on our minds
And our looks begin to change;
We develop new ways and opinions,
Because our course has come around
Those headlands that bedevilled us
And held us back upon our voyage.

The man has never come into this world
And nor will he ever come —
No matter how short his time may be
Should his eye see the day at all —
Who suffers no worldly distress
In the midst of success and love,
For no matter how swift be our voyage
It's in death we receive our reward.

If we get a reasonable number of years
Before we're asked to go over,
Difficulty and confusion
And anxiety will affect us;
Rust will set in from paralysis
And high spirits will be lost —
Our minds will be set in a groove,
Confused and lacking in joy.

Often do we look back
On the idea we had when we were young
(When we spent our time in blethering)
That no winter would ever afflict us:

Bha buailtean gorma 's raointean
  Ann am faoineasan na h-òig'
Gun smaoin air gaoth an eara-dheas
  Far na fairge dol thighinn òirnn.

Na caistealan gun d'dhìrich iad
  Le stìopaill do na speur'
Gun stéidhe-bhuinn ro chinnteach
  Mar a dh'innseas dhuinn an sgeul!
An-diugh chan fhaic mi sgeul orra,
  Sann thuit iad sìos gu léir —
Ged b' iol-cheàrnach 'n cuid sheòmraichean
  Si chòinneach nach do thréig.

Nuair chì mi madainn bhòidheach
  Bheir i m' òig' thugam as ùr
'S mi cuimhneachadh nan sòlasan
  'S cho bòidheach 's a bha gach flùr;
Ach thàinig tuiltean geamhraidh
  A chuir loinn nan crann fo smùr
'S cha léir dhomh nis ach sìorraidheachd
  Is crìonadh anns an ùir.

An Uibhist ghorm nan stùcan
  Far 'm bu dùthchasach an ceòl
A dh'fhosgail mi mo shùilean —
  Toiseach dùdlachd madainn m' òig';
'S ged dh'fhàiltich sneachd' a' gheamhraidh mi
  Aig doras gleann nan deòir,
Bha slàn-lusan is cluarain ann
  Nach mill gaoth tuath no reòdh.

Soraidh leat, a leughadair,
  'S na ruith leat fhéin don chùil —
Cha teich thu air an t-sìorraidheachd,
  Si 'chrìoch agad co-dhiù;
Gheibh am bàs a chòirichean
  (Tha 'n t-òrdagh aig' on chrùn)
Nuair dh'àithneas Rìgh na Glòrach
  A tha còmhnaidh os ar cionn.

Such green pastures and fields
Were but the vanities of youth
Without the thought of the south-east wind
That would blow on us off the sea.

How those castles rose up
With towers to the skies
Without too sure a foundation
As we're told by the tale!
I see no trace of them today,
For they have all fallen down —
Though their rooms had many corners
The moss hasn't left them alone.

When I see a beautiful morning
It brings me back to my youth
And I remember the pleasures
And how lovely was each flower;
But the floods of winter arrived
Which obscured the shape of the trees
And all I see now is eternity
And rotting in the grave.

It's in blue-green Uist of the mountains
Where music was in people's blood
That I first opened my eyes —
Early doldrums the dawn of my youth;
And though winter snow was my welcome
At the door of the valley of tears,
There were healing plants and thistles
Which no north wind or frost can destroy.

Farewell to you, dear reader,
And don't run to hide in a corner —
You can't escape eternity,
It's your destiny whatever;
Death will obtain his rights
(He has a mandate from the crown)
When the King of Glory commands
Who dwells above our heads.

Sgeulachdan nan Taighean-Céilidh

Ged a shéideadh faoilteach oirnn
Is faobhar nan gaoth tuath,
Ged bhiodh an sneachd' a' taosgadh
'S 'na stac ri taobh nam bruach,
Ged reothadh i mar stàilinn
Gu mullach àrd nan cruach,
Cha chumadh siud bhon chéilidh sinn
Far 'n cluinnte sgeul is duan.

Ged shileadh i gu dìorrasach
Le frasan fiadhaich fuar'
'S clach-mheallain tighinn bhon iarmailt
Ga siabadh oirnn mun cuairt,
Cha chumadh tuil no dìle sinn
'S cha bhiodh oirnn sgìths no gruaim
'S na h-eachdraidhean gan innse dhuinn
Le seanchaidh sìtheil suairc.

Bhiodh sloinneadh air ar sinnsearachd
Ga mhìneachadh 's ga luaidh,
Bhiodh deasbad air an iasgach ann,
'S gach deacair bha 'na ruaig;
Bhiodh tubaistean is bàthadh,
Is gàbhaidhean a' chuain,
'S bhiodh ionndrainn air na càirdean ann
Thug tuinn an t-sàile bhuainn.

Bhiodh Cogadh Mór a' Cheusair
Le chuid chreuchdan is mì-stàth,
A dh'fhàg na ceudan mìle
Ann an ìobradh fuar a' bhàis;
'Na sheanchas dh'fhàgadh leòinte sinn,
'S bu tric thug deòir 'nar pàirt
A' cuimhneachadh a' chòmhlain sin
A thréig an deò sna blàir.

The Tales of the Ceilidh-Houses

Even if wolftime were blowing on us
    And the keen blade of the northerlies,
Even if snow were cascading down
    And piling up on the hillsides,
Even if frost were as hard as steel
    Up to the high tops of the stacks,
It wouldn't keep us from the ceilidh
    Where story and song could be heard.

Even in torrential rain
    Full of cold squally showers
With hailstones coming from the sky
    Being swept round about us,
No flood or downpour kept us back
    Nor did we feel tired or gloomy
As we were being told stories
    By some calm competent reciter.

Our ancestral genealogy
    Would be set out and explained,
There'd be a debate about fishing
    And the difficulties besetting it;
There'd be accidents and drownings
    And the perils of the ocean,
And we'd remember the kinsfolk
    Of whom the sea waves had robbed us.

There'd be the Great War of the Kaiser
    With all its wounds and pointlessness,
Leaving hundreds of thousands
    In death's cold sacrifice;
It made us anguished to hear it,
    And our tears frequently flowed
As we remembered the many
    Who lost their lives in the battlefields.

Chluinnte sgeul bhiodh sònraichte
    Aig seòladair a' chuain,
A-muigh air bhàrr nam bòc-thonnan
    Ri aimsir reòdhta 's fhuar,
A' dìreadh do na h-àrd-chroinn
    'S a' teàrnadh asta nuas
'S an iùbhrach dol gu dùbhlan
    Ann an dùrantachd nan stuadh.

Bhiodh birlinnean MhicDhòmhnaill
    Le'n cuid sheòl a' dol gu sàil,
A' fàgail bun Loch Aoineart
    Le soills' na madainn thràth,
A' seòladh tro Chaol Ìle
    Ri aimsir iargalt' gràic
Gu fasgadh Carraig Fhearghais,
    Mar chaidh ainmeachas san dàn.

A-muigh air bhàrr Cuan Éirinn
    'S muir ag éirigh do na neòil,
Bhiodh Mac Nìll cur bhréid rith'
    Gu reubadh nan tonn mòr';
Cha chumadh aimsir Ruairidh
    An àm ceangal cruaidh nan ròp —
Bu Tartar anns a' chruadal e
    An àm cur suas nan seòl.

Bhiodh bòcain agus sìthich
    A' tuineadh cinnteach feadh nam bruach —
Bha iomadh sgeul ri inns' orra
    San tìm a chaidh air ruaig;
Bhiodh iad tric ri fàth-feith
    'S 'nan aincheist don an t-sluagh,
A' cur geas air pàistean
    'S a' cur mhàthraichean fo ghruaim.

Chluinnte sgeul mun àirigh
    Is mun mhànran is an ceòl
A bha cho tric a' tàrmachadh
    Am measg nan àlach òg';

Some special tale would be heard
From the sailor of the sea,
Out on top of the swelling waves
In cold freezing weather,
Climbing into the high masts
And climbing down them again
As the ship faced a challenge
Amongst the obdurate breakers.

The birlinns of MacDonald
Would put to sea fully rigged,
Leaving Loch Eynort's mouth
In the early morning light,
Sailing through Islay's Sound
In harsh inclement weather
To Carrickfergus's shelter
As described in the poem.[5]

Out on the height of the Irish Sea
With ocean rising to the clouds,
MacNeil would lay on more sail
For tearing the great waves;
No weather could stop Ruairi
In time of lashing the ropes —
He was a Tartar for toughness
When it came to hoisting sails.[6]

Ghosts and fairies most certainly
Dwelt amongst the braes —
Many tales would be told of them
In times now gone by;
They often lay in wait
And caused folk much trouble,
Placing spells upon the children
And worrying the mothers.

There'd be a tale of the shieling
And of the fun and music
That were so often pursued
By the younger generations;

Bhiodh tàin ann air am buachailleachd
A-muigh feadh chluaintean feòir —
Bha saorsa 's sìth neo-bhuaireasach
A' cuartachadh nan crò.

Dh'fhalbh na taighean càirdeil ud,
'S 'nan àit' tha gnàthach' ùr
'S tha mhuinntir bha gam pàirteachadh
An-diugh a' cnàmh san ùir;
Tha dòighean eil' air tàrmachadh
'S tha 'n abhcaideachd air chùl,
'S tha fàrdaichean an t-sòlais ud
'S an còmhlaichean 's iad dùint'.

Taigh Tasgaidh Chill Donnain

Mìle fàilt' air an aitribh 's air gach neach a chuir suas i,
Bidh i againn mar dhìleab bhios prìseil is luachmhor:
Chì sinn dealbhan ar càirdean a tha cnàmh anns na h-uaighean,
Chì sinn saothair an làmhan dearbhadh ànraidh is cruaidh-chàis.

Chì sinn innean na ceàrdaich far 'n d'rinneadh tàthadh 's faobhar,
Chì sinn geamhlag a' chlachair 's òrd bàrraidh an t-saoir ann;
Chì sinn làmh-cheàird a' ghreusaich' ('s gur brèagha 'chuid shaothrach)
Agus meuran an tàilleir a' cur na snàthaid troimhn aodach.

Tha iomadh cuimhneachan àraid san àit' seo fo'r còmhair
A' toirt eachdraidh ar sinnsear anns na tìmean air fògairt:
Tha 'n crann treabhaidh 's a' chliath ann, an criathar 's an t-sùiste,
'S tha acfhainn nan steud ann, bann-bràghad agus cruipean.

Tha 'chuidheall-shnìomha 's an càrd ann, agus brà-bhleith an eòrna,
Tha 'n spaid 's an gràp' ann, 's tha ràcan an fheòir ann;
Tha casan an fhéidh ann rinn ioma ceum feadh na mòintich
'S gunna dùbailt' an t-sealgair bu tric shealbhaich a bheòshlaint'.

Cattle would be herded there
  Out around the pastures —
Untroubled peace and freedom
  Encompassed the cowfolds.

Those friendly houses have gone,
  And new customs have replaced them
While the people who shared them
  Now rot in the soil;
Other ways have taken hold
  And such entertainment has gone,
While those buildings of pleasure
  Have had their doors all closed.

The Kildonan Museum

A thousand welcomes to the building and to all who have created it,
We will have it as a legacy that's precious and invaluable:
We'll see pictures of our kinsfolk who're decaying in their graves,
We'll see the produce of their hands as proof of hard times and adversity.

We'll see the anvil from the smithy where joints and edges were made,
We'll see the mason's crowbar and the joiner's hammer for nailing;
We'll see the shoemaker's handiwork (and lovely is his product)
While the thimble of the tailor put the needle through the clothes.

Many rare mementos in this place in front of us
Display the story of our ancestors in times now long gone by:
There's the plough and the harrow here, the riddle and the flail,
And there is horses' harness here, a collar-band and crupper.

The spinning-wheel and card are here, and the quern for grinding barley,
The spade and the graip are here, and the rake for the hay;
The antlers of the deer are here which made many mountain paths
And the hunter's double-barrelled gun which often furnished his livelihood.

Seann Taigh-Solais Chalbhaigh

Mìle beannachd dhut, a charaid,
  Tighinn gu carraig air nach eòl thu,
'S ma tha amaideas 'nad ghiùlain
  Cuiridh ùine sin air fògair;
Ma nì thu seasamh ann ceud bliadhna
  Nì thu liathadh mar as còir dhut,
Is nochdaidh tonnan a' Chuain Sgìth dhut
  Nach ann gun strì gheibh thu do bheòshlaint.

Ged a tha thu òg is làidir
  'S mòran chàirdean air do chùlaibh,
S iomadh oidhche 's là thig éiginn
  Nuair bhios séideadh air na dùilean,
Nuair a chopas tuinn na mara
  Tighinn 'nan steallan geala tùillich —
Cuimhnichidh tu orm an uair sin
  'S air gach cruas a bha 'nam dhùnach.

S iomadh oidhche ghruamach geamhraidh
  Thug mi gealltainn agus dòchas
Do mharaiche nan tonnan uaine
  Bhiodh air bhàrr a' chuain a' seòladh;
An uair a shéideadh i bhon iar-dheas
  Le frasan dìorrais air bheag tròcair,
S tric a rinn mo sholas iùil dhaibh
  'S e toirt an cùrsaireachd gu òrdagh.

Na dìochuimhnich a' ghruagach
  Air a bheil an cuailean òrbhuidh':
S tric a smaointean is a bruadar
  Air na tonnan uaine cròiceach;
S tric bhios iomchoir' 'na gluasad
  Nuair thig séideadh cruaidh bho Aeòlas —
Se dh'fhàg 'na h-aonar anns an uair i
  Gun tug i luaidh do dh'fhear an t-seòlaidh.

The Old Lighthouse of Calvay

A thousand welcomes, my friend,
  Coming to unfamiliar landing-rock,
And if there's daftness in your manner
  Time will soon put paid to that;
If you stand a hundred years on it
  You'll go grey as you ought to,
And the Minch's waves will show you
  You won't earn your living easily.

Though you're young and resilient
  With many relatives behind you,
There'll be many nights and days of crisis
  When the elements start blowing,
When the waves break into foam
  And come in white spouts of spindrift —
You will think of me then
  And of all the strength in my fortress.

On many surly winter nights
  I gave promise, I gave hope
To the mariner of pale green waves
  Who'd be sailing the high seas;
When it blew sou'westerly
  With angry showers of little mercy,
My light so often guided them
  And corrected their course.

Don't forget the girl
  With the golden head of hair:
Often are her thoughts and dreams
  On the foaming pale-green waves;
There's frequent anger in her step
  When a blast comes from Æolus —
What's now left her on her own
  Is giving love to a sailor.
The fishermen, it's well I knew them,

B' eòlach mi air luchd an iasgaich,
  Bha iad riamh an-seo 'nam nàbachd:
B' eòlach mi air Raghnall mac Iagain
  'S am bàta brèagh' aige, *Naomh Pàdraig*;
Nuair nochdadh i far Rubh' na h-Òrdaig
  Si bha bòidheach air an t-sàile —
Chan fhaca mi ré mo shaoghail
  Dol tro chaolas té cho àlainn.

Bha mi eòlach air na daoin' ud,
  Bhiodh iad daonnan tighinn 'nam chàirdeas:
S duilich leam a bhith smaointinn
  Nach fhaic a h-aon aca mi fàgail;
Rinn am feasgar aca ciaradh,
  Chaidh an grian-san sìos air fàire —
Tha iad ann an suain nan sìorraidh
  Is tuinn a' Chuain an-Iar gan tàladh.

Chunnaic mi tric a' falbh iad,
  Gillean calma, smiorail, làidir,
Maighdeannan is mnathan òg'
  A' dol air fògradh thar an t-sàile;
S mi bhiodh muladach gan ionndrainn
  Agus tùrsach gun do dh'fhàg iad —
'S bha mi ann a-seo nuair thill iad
  Ged, mo chreach, nach d'thill ach pàirt dhiubh.

Nam biodh m' eachdraidh air a h-innse
  Ann am mìneachadh clò-bhualaidh,
Bhiodh luchd aithris agus sgrìobhaidh
  Ann an iomartais a buannachd:
Tha mi ùine mhór san t-saoghal
  'S chan ann aotrom bhios mo chnuasachd —
Tha mo chomasan cho àraid,
  Dh'ionnsaich farpaisean a' chuain mi.

Chunnaic mi ri ruith nam bliadhna
  Iomadh iorghaill agus còmhrag,
Dh'fhiosraich mi dà Chog' an t-Saoghail
  'S anns gach aon dhiubh ghabh mi cò-phàirt;

They were always here around me:
Raghnall mac Iagain, well I knew him
And his fine boat, the *St Patrick*;[7]
When she'd appear off Rubh' na h-Òrdaig
She was beautiful on the ocean —
I've never seen in all my life
A boat as fine going through narrows.

Those men, it's well I knew them,
They would always come to see me:
It's hard for me to understand
That none of them will see me leave;
Dusk has fallen on them all,
Their sun's gone down on the horizon —
They've gone to their eternal rest
With Atlantic waves crooning them.

I've so often seen them go,
Brave lads, strong and substantial,
Girls and young married women
Going to exile overseas;
I was sad because I missed them
And depressed that they had left —
And I was here when they returned
Though only some, alas, came back.

Should the story of my life be told
In some printed publication,
Historians and other writers
Would greatly benefit from it:
I'm a long time in the world
And my reflections won't be light —
My powers are so particular,
I've been tried by ocean conflicts.

I have seen through the years
Many contests and struggles,
I've experienced the two World Wars
And taken part in each of them;
My duties I've performed

Chaidh mo dhleasnais a dhearbhadh,
   Cha robh cearbaiche 'nam dhòighean —
Chan eil ailisean ri'm fàgail
   No ri'n càrnadh aig mo chòmhlaidh.

Mìle beannachd le gach caraid
   Bha cho daingeann air mo chùlaibh,
Gu h-àraid Lachlainn Mór MacCoinnich,
   Fear cho sgoinneil 's tha san dùthaich:
Bha e math dhomh 'n réis nam bliadhna
   Ann an tèarainteachd is cùram —
Guma fada fallain slàn e
   Tighinn don àite seo gad ionnsaigh.

Ach a-nis bhon thàinig caochladh
   Nì mi saod air a bhith gluasad,
Fhuair mi airgead na h-aoise
   'S tha mo shaors' air a buannachd;
Théid mi cuairt am measg nan còmhlan
   'S fàiltichidh mi le deòin is suairc' iad —
'S cha lorg iad aineolas 'nam chòmhradh
   Ged a ruiginn bòrd nan uaislean!

NOTES

1 (p. 3) Donald John MacDonald's poetry was published by Club Leabhar, Inverness, as *Sguaban Eòrna* ('Barley Sheaves') in 1973, and reissued by Birlinn with Bill Innes's English translations as *Chì Mi* in 1998.

2 (p. 3) Donald John MacDonald spent the years 1940–45 as a prisoner of war in Germany. His graphic account of his experiences appeared as *Fo Sgàil a' Swastika* (Club Leabhar, Inverness, 1974) and was reissued under the same title by Acair of Stornoway in 2000 with an English translation by Bill Innes.

3 (p. 3) *Sguaban Eòrna* contains, at pp. 99 and 101, poems to Mòrag and

With no sloppiness of method —
No reproaches remain
Or lie stacked up at my door.

A thousand farewells to each friend
Who was so staunch behind me,
Especially Big Lachlan MacKenzie,
As fine a man as any in the land:
He was good to me through all those years
In security and care —
May he long keep his health and strength
To come here and visit you.

But now since change has come
I'll get ready and go,
I have the old age pension
And my freedom is won;
I'll go and mingle with the crowd
And greet them gladly and politely —
Nor will they find my talk ignorant
Should I even reach the top people's table!

Notes

Maighread Òg.

4 (p. 3) A reference to the poem 'Taigh a' Bhàird' ('The Poet's House'), for which see *Chì Mi* p. 260, *An Tuil* p. 424.

5 (p. 71) 'Birlinn Chlann Raghnaill' ('Clanranald's Galley') by Alexander MacDonald, *Alastair mac Mhaighstir Alastair* (*c.* 1698 – *c.* 1770).

6 (p. 71) *Ruairidh an Tartair*, a MacNeil warrior who lived around 1600. His name actually means 'Ruairi of the Big Noise' but the poet takes advantage of the double meaning of 'tartar'.

7 (p. 77) Ronald Macmillan.

A' Ghàidhlig

Cànain thaitneach inntinneach a dh'ionnsaich mi 'nam òig'
'S a-chaoidh gu bràch nach dìobair mi gu'n sìnear mi fon fhòd:
Ged tha mo Bheurla dì-neartach, 's gun mhòran brìgh no treòir,
Cha dèan a gainne dìteadh dhomh 'nam chuairt an tìr nam beò.

Tha Ghàidhlig neartmhor ùmailteach is math an cùirt an t-sluaigh,
Tha i fonnmhor meadrachais gu mùigeachd chur air ruaig;
Tha puing a ciùil cho brìoghmhor 's cho sìtheil tighinn gu d' chluais
Gun tàlaidh i an trom-inntinneach gu sàmhchair tìr na suain.

An uair a thig an deacaireachd 's an riasladh mar as dual
Thig furtachd gu ar crìochan le seanchas diadhaidh suairc;
Tha còmhradh ciùin sa Ghàidhlig don ànrach sa chàs-chruaidh
Mar sholas iùil don t-seòladair air bòc-thonnan a' chuain.

Bha am fiosaiche ag ràdha gun robh Ghàidhlig aig na h-eòin,
Gun robh 'n lon-dubh ri bàrdachd 's a' filleadh dhàn an clò,
'S 'nar beachdaireachd gheurchuiseach ri còisir eun sna neòil
Gun cluinn sinn fuinn na Gàidhlig 'nan cuid àbhachdais is ceòl!

Chan iongnadh leam a' Ghàidhlig a bhith tàrmachadh 'nam smuain
A liuthad oidhche a dh'éist mi ris na sgeulachdan 's na duain
Aig bodaich chalma liath-cheannach 's gur crìon tha iad san uaigh —
Fois is sìth na sìorraidh dhaibh, is sàmhchair ciat' bith-bhuan.

A' Ghaoth an-Iar tha Séideadh thar na Mara

A' ghaoth an-iar tha séideadh thar na mara
A-nall bho dhùthaich bheairteach Tìr nan Craobh,
An inn's thu sgeul dhuinn mun mhuinntir a chaidh thairis
'S a thriall air astar fada troimh na caoil?

An do dh'ionndrainn iad an càirdean is an dachaigh,
Na glinn agus na machraichean 's na raoin,
Na cluaintean san do ghluais iad òg le caithream
Gun smaointean ac' air earras no air maoin?

Na cnuic agus na gnobain uaine chorrach
Far 'm bòidheach dh'fhàsas raineach air gach taobh,
Far 'm faic sinn cluaran-deilgneach air a' mhonadh
'S far an tàmh le sonas a' chearc-fhraoich?

Far 'n cluinn sinn ceòl na cuthaig anns a' chéitean
Nuair thilleas i gu Éiseabhal nan stùc:
Gheibh i mìle fàilt' bho shean is òg ann
'S i beòthachadh ar dòchas dhuinn as ùr.

Bu tric a dh'éist an cluas ri gàir na mara
Nuair bhristeadh tonnan geala feadh na tiùrr —
Na tuinn sin rinn an giùlain fad' bho'n eòlas
Nuair sheòl iad orr' 'nam fògarraich a-null.

Bha dìsle ann an tathaich an taigh-chéilidh
Far an cluinneadh iad na sgeulachdan 's na duain,
Far na dh'fhiosraich iad an coibhneas anns a' chòmhradh
Mu chagailtean an t-sòlais mar bu dual.

Far 'n cluinneadh iad na h-eachdraidhean gan innse,
Gach facal air a mhìneachadh dha'n cluais —
Shloinneadh iad an càirdeas is an sinnsear,
A' meòmhrachadh air tìmean fad' air ruaig.

Sheòl iad fada bhuainn air tuinn an t-sàile
'S dh'fhàg iad tìr a' chrà-gheòidh as an déidh
Far 'n éisteadh iad ri ceòlraidh ghrinn na Gàidhlig
Ri taobh a' ghealbhain bhlàith 'nan dachaigh fhéin.

Far 'n cluinneadh iad an smeòrach anns a' mhadainn
'S an uiseag aotrom ealanta toirt sunnd,
Guileag eala bhàin a' snàmh air locha
Is earrach eil' air teachd gu tìr an fhraoich.

Am Faoilteach 1984

Dh'fhalbh an geamhradh neo-aoigheil,
Dh'fhalbh am faoilteach 's an dùbhlachd,
Dh'fhalbh aimsir na dochair
A thug iomadh leòn air an dùthaich;
Thàinig sìth agus sìochaint
Mar thoirbheart tiodhlaic an ungaidh
A chuireas bruansgath nan sìontan
Le am farpais fhiadhaich air chùlaibh.

Thàinig sìth agus saorsainn
'S thill aoibh agus sòlas,
Shearg connspaid na truaighe
Nuair dh'fhalbh am fuachd 's a' ghaoth-reòdhta;
Thàinig teachdair' an t-sùgraidh
A chuireas sunnd sean is òg oirnn,
'S théid air dìochuimhn' gach bruaillean
'S bidh 'n cadal luasgain nas stòlda.

Thig bàidh agus coibhneas
'S thig aoibhneas gu'r n-ionnsaigh,
Thig deàlradh na gréine
Thar sléibhtean is stùcan;
Bidh ealtainn na h-iarmailt
A' seinn le ciatachd a' chiùil dhuinn,
A' toirt moladh don Àrdrigh
A thug iad sàbhailt' troimh dhùbhlan.

Bidh cuimhn' air an fhaoilteach
'S air a' ghaoid rinn e fhàgail
Fads bhios fairge nam brùchd-thonn
Tighinn gu tiùrra na tràghad;
Bidh eachdraidh na deuchainn
Ann am briathran 'na athailt
Mu thoiseach na bliadhn' ud
A leum thar crìochan na h-àbhaist.

An Sgurra Beag

Air cliathach Éiseabhail chorraich far bheil fraoch agus borran ri fàsachd,
Far 'm bi chuach anns a' Chéitean le fonn na féin-thoil cur fàilt' oirnn,
Tha Sgurra Beag nan creag chiar-chas air stéidh iarnaidh nach fàilnich
'S ged a shéideadh na sìontan cha toir iad iargain no tàir dhut.

Tha thu ann troimh na linntean 's chum thu 'n t-sìth 's an t-sàmhchair —
Cha chluinn mi iomradh san tìr air thu bhith strì ri do nàbaidh;
Ged rachadh coigreach neo-dhligheachais thar do chrìche le dànachd,
Sann le deagh ghean is dìlse a théid da-rìreadh an fhàilt' air.

Ged tha thu carraigeach duaichnidh 's coltas gruamach air t' aodann,
Tha thu seasmhach gun truailleachd agus stuama gun aomadh;
Chan eil lag-bheirt ri luaidh ort ré do chuairt anns an t-saoghal,
'S ma tha dubhach 'nad ghruaidhean tha gaol is uaisle 'nad smaointean.

Tha fraoch badanach bòidheach mu do chòsagan àrsaidh
Tha 'na shuaicheantas sònraicht' aig Clann Dòmhnaill nam blàth-chridh':
Freumh dìleas is fosgarrach sliochd oirbheirt na dànadais —
'S bidh an ainm ann am beòthalachd fhads bhios cròic air na gàir-thonnan.

Anns a' mhadainn bidh 'n eunlaith le fuinn bhriagha cur fàilt' ort,
A' toirt moladh dhan Trianaid a thug dìon fo do sgàil dhaibh,
A chum iad sàbhailt' bhon dìorras is aimsir fhiadhaich no ascaoin
'S a rinn an aiseag le mìorbhail troimh dhoineann ìargaill no gàbhadh.

Gheibh iad fasgadh is aoigheachd am measg fraoidhnidh na bòidhche
'S nì iad cadal gu saor a dh'ainneoin gaoirich na dòbhaidh:
Iad 'nan suain anns an tèarainteachd am measg do chiar-chreagan ròcach —
Roghainn dachaigh an sgiathair a théid fo dhìon anns a' ghlomhais.

Chì mi seallaidh tha ciatach 's a nì leudachd dha m' eòlas,
Chì mi tabh nan tonn iargaill far 'n dèan an t-iasgair a bheòshlaint;
Chì mi Chuiltheann tha ianach 's bùird mhìorbhail MhicLeòid bhuat
'S chì mi loingeas chrann àrda air muir ghàbhaidh a' seòladh.

Ged as coimheach bhios t' aogas an àm faoilteach a' bhuairidh
Thig an samhradh le chaoine a' cur aoibh air do ghruaidhean;
Bidh do chòmhdach cho rìomhach ri còta sìod' na ban-dubhairiche
'S ann an deasbad na dìreachais cha bhi mi 'n nòs ri luaidh ort.

Cluaintean Éiseabhail

Gur bòidheach cluaintean Éiseabhail nuair thig an céitean òirnn,
Nuair thig a' chuthag dhubh-ghorm le loinn is sunnd is ceòl;
Air dìochuimhn' théid an dùbhlachd is aimsir dhuibhre reòdht',
'S bidh grian nan speur gar fàilteachadh le neart is càil is treòir.

Ged nach fàs na craobhan ort tha pailteas fraoich mu d' bhruaich,
Chì sinn lusan maothalach gach taobh a théid sinn cuairt:
Bidh 'n t-sòbhrag òrbhuidh rìomhach 'na mìltean feadh nan cluan
'S bidh canach geal nan sléibhtean 'nan éideadh dhut gun uaill.

Air feasgair chiùin san t-samhradh bidh fann-ghuth tighinn gu m' chluais
Aig monmhair cheòlmhor aibhnichean a' triall 'nan deann gu cuan;
Bidh seillean ruadh is srann aige a' deoghal phlannt nam bruach,
A' càrnadh stòr a' gheamhraidh nuair thig teannach' na gaoith tuath.

Bidh iomadh seòrsa flùran bho d' bhonn gu d' chrùn a' fàs,
Bidh neòineinean is dìtheanan a' cinntinn mu do bhlàir;
Bidh frìth-raineach is luachair a' cuartachadh do shàil
'S bidh cluaran uaine frìth-bhacach 'na dhìleab dhut gu bràch.

Tha cluaintean fasgach feurach ort 's thu fialaidh ann mu'm pàirt,
Tha sgòrran seasgair tèarainte aig eunlaith air son tàmh;
Gheibh iad cadal aoibhneach troimhn oidhche fo a sgàil,
Toirt taingealais nuair dhùisgeas iad le cur an ciùil an àird.

Is iomadh eun nì tàmhadh le càirdeas feadh do bhruaich —
Bidh smeòrach ghlas san òg-mhadainn a' seinn a ceòl 's a duan,
Bidh 'n uiseag anns na speuran cho réidh ag éirigh suas,
Cur mìle fàilt' air Éiseabhal nan glaic 's nan réidhlean uain'.

An t-Seann Chaora

Sann am Muile nam fuar-bheann
A dh'àraicheadh suas thu 'nad òig' —
Eilean àlainn nan cluaintean
'S nan cas-bheanntan uaine fo cheò
Far bheil creachadh an fhuadaich
Ann an eachdraidh bhios buan ann an clò
Fhads bhios gairge nan stuadhan
A' bristeadh le nuallan mu 'chòrs.

Bhon bha gluasad 'nad nàdar
Dh'fhàg thu gorm-eilean t' àraich air chùl
'S ghabh thu d' aiseag gu sàbhailt',
Tro Chaol Mhuile ann am bàta na smùid;
Sann air Uibhist nan crà-ghèadh
A rinn thu gu dàna do chùrs',
'S cha do dh'iarr thu gus fhàgail
Gu'n deach do thiodhlacadh sàmhach 'na ùir.

Fhuair thu bliadhnaichean saoghail
Nach eil tric air a shaoradh dha d' sheòrs':
Dh'fhàg siud eòlas aig daoin' ort
A dh'fhiosraich 'nad aois thu 's 'nad òig';
Bha chlann bheag ort cho déidheil,
Se bhith 'nad chuideachd a b' aoibhneas dha'n dòigh —
Bha togail inntinn cho dlùth dhaibh,
'S bha d' asgaillean lùthmhor dha d' fheòil.

Dh'fhàg thu cuimhneachain éibhinn
A bhios am pàirteachas déine mo smuain,
Thug thu deas-ghnàth dha m' inntinn
A chuir gnùis-bhrat na mùigeachd air ruaig;
Tha gach nàbaidh gad ionndrainn,
Cha robh naimhdeas no diombadh 'nad chuairt,
'S gum bu lìonmhor na flùran
Bhios 'nan àilleachd a' brùchdadh mu d' uaigh.

Angela

Tha rìbhinn bhòidheach air tighinn as ùr oirnn:
    Thug i sunnd agus sùgradh dhòmhsa
Mar ghathan gréine air uchd nan speuran
    A' fuadach éislein air sgéith an fhògairt.

Ged s àghmhor dìtheinean Beinn Parnassus
    Bidh ainm an àilleachd gu bràch ri còmhradh:
A-cheart cho rìomhach tha blàth do shnuaidh-sa —
    Tha h-uile buaidh ort as dual do dh'òg-bhean.

Chan eil flùr a nì fàs san t-samhradh
    A nì samhladh dhut ann am bòidhchead
Mar shòbhrag mhìn-bhuidh' ri taobh an alltain
    'S grian na Bealltainn le geall ga h-òradh.

Mar dhreach an lon duibh am measg nan cléiteag
    Tha d' fhalt cho réidh ann an cumadh òrdail;
Tha blàths an t-samhraidh a' snàmh 'nad ghruaidhean
    'S tha mhil ga suaineadh an snuadh do bhòidhche.

Mar reul a' deàrrsadh air bhàrr na h-iarmailt
    Nuair nì a' ghrian a dhol sìos fo sgòthan;
Mar dhealt a' boillsgeadh cho ciatach rùnach
    Sa mhadainn ùir am measg fhlùr is ròsan.

Do dheud cho geal ri sneachd san dùbhlachd
    An glaic is stùc ann am meadhan mòintich,
Mar fhaoilinn bhàn bhios air bhàrr an t-srùthlaidh
    Am mealadh sùgraidh air crùn nam bòc-thonn.

Guma slàn a bhitheas tu san dùthaich
    Gu cridheil sunndach an Gleann na Ceòlraidh —
Do chadal suaineach air cluasaig chaoin-ghil
    'S do dhùsgadh saodmhor le gaol is sòlas.

Ar Crìoch

Se 'n cladh 's an uaigh an dachaigh bhuan,
Crìoch ar cuairt air thalamh —
Sa ghainmhich fhuair, paisgte suas
Measg bhòrdan cruaidhe 's anairt.

Cha chluinn sinn onfhadh aig a' ghaoith
A' cuimhleadh feadh a' mhachair,
Cha chluinn sinn monmhair thonn air tràigh
Bhon dh'fhalbh gu bràch ar caithris.

Socair sàmhach anns an ùir
Tha dùthchasach dha'r cnàimhean,
Cha dèan an eunlaith le'n cruit-chiùil
Ar dùsgadh anns a' mhadainn.

A chuid chaidh seachran air uaigh
Tha doimhn' a' chuain a' falach —
Cha bhi iad leithreachais air càch
Nuair théid na sgàilean seachad.

Chì Mi Bhuam

Chì mi bhuam, chì mi bhuam,
Chì mi bhuam ann na seallaidh —
Chì mi monaidhean fo fhraoch,
Chì mi aonaich is bealaich.

'Na mo shuidh' air mullach stùc
Anns an ùr-mhadainn earraich
Chì mi seallaidh ann mun cuairt
A bheir suairceas gu m' aire.

Chì mi Hiort a-muigh san iar,
Dachaigh eunlaith na mara,
Cath ri tonnan glas' a' chuain
Nuair thig luasgan sa ghaillinn.

Chì mi Éirisgeigh nam flùr,
  Chì mi null Eilean Bharraigh;
Chì mi Chuiltheann 's Bùird MhicLeòid —
  S tric na sgòthan gam falach.

Chì mi beanntan creagach Rùm,
  'S air a chùl Eilean Chanaigh;
Chì mi Tiriodh ghorm nan cluan —
  Tìr bu dual do luchd-ealain.

Chì mi mainnireach chruidh-laoigh
  Air gach taobh anns a' mhonadh,
Cuimhneachain na tìm a bhà —
  Measgadh càs agus sonais.

Chì mi aibhnichean 'nan still
  Triall troimh ghlinn chun a' chladaich,
Chì mi eunlaith air an sgéith
  Cur air ghleus an cuid caithreim.

Chì mi guilbnich agus naoisg,
  Cearcan fraoich agus lachainn,
'S air gach bealach chì mi chuach
  Tighinn thar chuantan gu'r n-amharc.

Chì mi churracag bhreac le sunnd
  Cur na smùid dhith san adhar,
Teachdaire nan roghainn sgeul
  G'eil 'nar déidh fuachd is gailleann.

Chì mi long a' dol troimh chaoil
  Cath ri gaoir-gheal na mara,
Gillean sunndach innt' air bòrd
  Dol thar bhòids' air an aineol.

Chì mi rìbhinn an fhuilt òir —
  S tric a bòidhchead air m' aire
'S i cho snuadhmhor ris an ròs
  Bhios fo òg-dhriùchd na madainn.

Chan eil Sinn gun Sùgradh

Chan eil sinn gun sùgradh sa cheàrn seo dhen dùthaich,
Bidh m' inntinn-sa dlùthadh gu sunndach gu ceòl
'S gun innis mi san duan dhuibh mu bhòidhche nan cluaintean
'S nan cas-ghleanntan uain' an do ghluais mi 'nam òig'.

Tha Éiseabhal stùcach le fraoch air a crùnadh
Toirt seallaidh dha m' shùil a bheir rùintean 'nam chòir;
Le aibhnichean luathais a' triall chun nan cuantan
'S nan garbh-thonnan uain' bhios a' sluaisreadh mun chòrs'.

Tha eunlaith nan speuran a' seinn air an sgéith ann
Le aiteas gun bheud ann an réidheachd 's an ceòl,
Ag itealaich sgèimheil cho bòidheach san iarmailt
'S a' caithream gu'm miann am measg riolainn is neòil.

Tha lochannan fìoruisg' aig bonn nam beann sìon-bhuailt',
Gur pailt lachainn riabhach ag iadhadh mun òb;
Tha am breac ann ri iasgach, gum faigh thu gu d' mhiann e —
'S gur taitneach am biadh e 's e riaraicht' air bòrd.

Nuair thig àm h-Éill Pàdraig is aimsir na h-àilleachd
Bidh dìtheanan àghmhor a' fàs feadh an fheòir;
Bidh 'n t-sòbhrag 's an cluaran ag òradh nan cluaintean
'S bidh ceileir na cuaich' mar as dual san t-seann nòs.

Ged a tha mi fàs aosta 's mo bheachdan air caochladh
Cha leig mi le baobhachd bhith 'g aomadh 'nam chòir,
Bidh subhachas daonnan ag iadhadh mo smaointean
'S bidh réimis gun daors' cumail faondradh air bròn.

An uair ghlacas am bàs mi aig deireadh mo làithean
Le carthannachd chàich théid mo chàramh fon fhòd
Ann an ìochdar Chnoc Hàllainn am fianais na tràigh-ghil
Far an caidil mi 'n sàmhchair am measg nàbaidhean m' òig'.

Creag na Cuthaig

Ge b'e có dhìreas ri aodann
Glaic an Daimh nan cruaidh-lusan,
Chì e sealladh dhen dùr-charraig ghròbaich
A sheas ris na dùilean,
'S don ghaillinn cha d'ùmhail —
'S cha d' chuir drannadh na dùbhlachd ort fògairt.

Cha d' chuir òglaidh' na tuath-ghaoith
Ana-ghoireas 'nad ghruaidhean
Ged a shéideadh i cruaidh ann an deòthais;
Tha thu teann air do stéidhe
'S don onagaid cha ghéill thu
Ged as tric bhios i geur-lean' le dòileas.

Tha thu daingeann air d' ùrlar
Le greim teann air a' ghrunndail
'S chan eil lapaich' na lughdaich' 'nad dhòrnan:
Tha thu foghainteach làidir
'S cha chuir aimsir glas-làmh ort
A dh'ainneoin seicleadh as ascaoin aig Aeòlus.

S iomadh geamhradh is faoilteach
Le'n cuid lann-ghathadh faobhrach
A thug ionnsaigh le gaorradh mu do sheòmair,
A' maoimeadh do stialladh
Is cur ás dhuit le'n dìorras,
Le anastachd fhiadhaich gun tròcair.

An uair a dh'fhalbhas an dùbhlan
'S aimsir aingidh na h-ùpraid
Bidh uallachas ùr mu do sheòmair,
Thig gathannan gréin' ort
Thar mullaich nan sléibhtean
'S bidh thu sgéithte le éideadh bhios glòrmhor.

Bheir an t-earrach dhuit ùire
Le cleòca dhe fhlùran
A chuireas dreach agus mùirneachd na h-òig' ort;
Bidh do thrusgan cho àillidh
Le dathan uain' agus sgàrlaid,
Bheir thu buaidh am measg chàich ann an òirdheirc'.

Bidh an t-sòbhrag chiùin mhàlda
Le aoibh a' cur fàilt' ort,
Bidh an cluaran a' fàs ann le cholgan;
Bidh dìtheanan briagha
Nan cuairteanan iadhshlait
'Nam brat-ùrlar air bhialaibh do chomhair.

Bidh eunlaith na h-àirde
Le ceòl a' cur fàilt' ort
Anns a' mhoch-mhadainn thràth 's anns a' ghlòmainn,
Bidh crònan a' chaochain
Air a thuras troimhn chaol-ghleann
Mar channtaireachd chaomhach na ceòlraidh.

Creag nan Sealbhag

'Na suidhe balbh neo-léirsinneach fo Éiseabhal nan stùc
Tha charraig ghruamach gheur-bhacach fo éideadh allaidh cùmt',
'S ge b'e có bhaist 'nad leanabas thu gun d' dhearbh e géire sùl'
Nuair thug e Creag nan Sealbhag ort — an t-ainm a dhearbh do chliù.

An uair thig bòidhchead samhraidh ort gun tilg thu 'ghreann ud bhuat,
Is nochdaidh tu gun d' phlanntaich thu air ais gu Bealltainn nuadh:
Beathaichidh an ùr-mhadainn gach flùr tha ort mun cuairt
Is sgeadaichidh an t-sealbhag thu le trusgan dealbhach uain'.

Cha spìocair thu 'nad sheòmraichean, tha cùirteas pailt 'nad phàirt,
Bidh cuirmean dhe gach seòrsa aig na h-eòin tha ort a' tàmh;
Bidh uiseagan is smeòraichean ri ceòl sa mhadainn thràth —
'S 'nam measg bidh guth na cuaiche tighinn air chuairt oirnn thar an t-sàil.

Tha fraoidhneas àlainn dhìtheinean air bàrr do chinn mar shròl,
Fàsaidh fail-chuach rìomhach ort is raineach rìoghail òg;
Bidh dris a' sreap ri d' chliathaichean gu smeur-phreasach le stòr
'S gur tric le inntinn shuaimhneach rinn mi 'm buain an làithean m' òig'.

Ged shéideadh gaoth na h-iarmailt gu dìorrasach on tuath
Cha ghiùlain thu còt'-ìochdair air son do dhìon on fhuachd;
Dh'fhàg cumhachd nàdair tèaraint' thu o shìontanan gun truas
'S ma dh'fhàg siud ann am fiachan thu gun phàigh thu riadh mar dhuais.

Tha ionaltradh aig caoraich 's crodh-laoigh a thig fo d' sgàth,
Do choibhneas cha tig caochladh air cho fads bhios fraoch mu d' bhàrr;
'S cho fads bhios ceò na h-iarmailt ag iadhadh ort mochthràth
Bidh salmadair nan sgiathan mu d' sgoran ciar' a' tàmh.

Ged a thriall na nàbaidhean bha tàmhachd ort mun cuairt
(Thug deireadh réis gu sàmhchair iad fo ùspairn sàradh cruaidh),
Bu tric a rinn iad sùgradh gu sùrdalach mu d' bhruaich
'S tha thusa 'n-siud mar dh'fhàg iad thu fo sgàil nan toman uain'.

Fuaim an t-Sàile

Chan eil ceòl a thig gu m' chluasan
As binne leam na fuaim an t-sàile,
Crònan iorghailleach an t-srùthlaidh
'S e ri diùbhrais air an tràigh ann.

Guth nan eilthireach ri chluinntinn
Anns na tuinn tighinn chun na tràghad,
Dùrachdan gan cur le dìlse
Chun na tìr' a rinn iad fhàgail.

Anns na briathran gheibh sinn mùrcais,
Gheibh sinn tùirse anns an fhàilte;
Gheibh sinn mulad anns an dùrachd —
Ionndrainn a tha dlùth do nàdar.

Ionndrainn air na cnuic 's na cluaintean
A tha dualach do gach nàistinn —
Far 'm bi freumhaichean ar dùthchais
Sann as dlùithe bhios ar càirdeas.

Far bheil freumhaichean an sinnsear
Far an deach sa chill an càramh,
Far 'n do chuireadh a' chiad ùir orr'
'S far an dùisg iad air là àraid.

Far 'm bu tric iad air an glùintean
Dèanamh ùrnaigh uile-ghràsmhor,
Far 'n do dh'ionnsaich iad gach ùmhlachd
Thug troimh iomadh cùis iad sàbhailt'.

Far an cual' iad iomadh sgeula
San taigh-chéilidh ann an nàbachd —
Comhairlean an t-seann duin' shìobhalt'
Air am mìneachadh gu bàidheil.

Bhon se annrath agus cruaidh-chàs
Chuir gu gluasad iad thar sàile,
S tric air ais a' tighinn an smuaintean
Far bheil sìth nam buadh is àiteas.

Maighdeann Ghrinn Loch Cheàrsanais

Si maighdeann ghrinn Loch Cheàrsanais a dhùisg an-dràst' mo cheòl
'S gun sgrìobh mi anns a' Ghàidhlig mu h-àilleachd is a bòidhch':
Gu sunndach loinneil rìomhach i 's i sìobhalta gun phròis
Mar ghathan blàth' gréine madainn chéitein a' tighinn òirnn.

Tha cridhealas an t-samhraidh 'nad ìomhaigh choibhneil chòir,
Mar dhealt air bhàrr nam flùran tha bilean rùin do cheòil;
Mar rionnag anns an iarmailt air oidhche bhriagha reòdht'
Tha deàrrsadh do shùilean a' toirt ar sùgradh beò.

Gur binne leam do chòmhradh na crònan uillt nam beann,
Cho fonnmhor ri smeòrach tha cur ceòlraidh feadh nan gleann;
Do dheud mar shneachd san fhaoilteach 's mar fhaoileag air bhàrr thonn
'S mar chanach ùr air mòintich nuair tha 'n t-Ògmhios a' tighinn teann.

Mar bhogha-frois san Lùnastail tighinn dlùth ri àm na buan'
Tha do chuailean rìomhach 's na cìrean dol 'na dhuail;
Tha aoibh is dreach tha sònraichte a' còmhdachadh do shnuaidh —
Gun dealbhaich mi 'nad bhòidhchead thu ri ròsan anns na cluain.

Loch Cheàrsanais

Gur lòghmhor ort dearcadh fo leargainn nam fuar-bheann
'S an ceò tighinn a-nuas ort bho ghuaillean na h-àird';
B'e roghainn fear sùl-bheachd bhith dlùth dha do bhruaichean —
B'e tiompanachd luachmhor dh'a chluasan bhith 'd phàirt.

Nuair a dh'éireas a' ghrian anns a' chiat'-mhadainn bhòidhich,
Cur sgàile na glòir ann an òr-bheirt a cuairt,
Cha cheil i do roinn ort, tha thu 'n oighreachd a còirean —
Mar a dhearbhas a' choirill aig na h-eòin mu do bhruaich.

Tha coimhcheangal cho làidir aig nàdar ri d' ghuaimeas
Fo fhàsgadh nam fuar-bheann is uaigneas nan gleann;
Gheibh eunlaith caomh-chàirdeas am fraoch-sgriachain do bhruachan:
Bho chunnart an turgain gheibh iad suaimhneas nach gann.

Bheir an lacha gu ìre le dìcheall a h-àlach,
Bidh an fhaoileag a' snàmh ort ri blàths agus fuachd;
Bidh chearc-uisg' tighinn far faicill gu trabhaich d' oirthire
'S gur tric corra-ghritheach le slìob-cheum mu d' bhruaich.

'N àm don ghealaich bhith 'g éirigh air réiteachd a cuairtean
'S i deàrrsadh a-nuas ort le buaidhean an àigh,
Bidh sàmhchair is sìochaint mu chrìochan Glaic Ruairidh
Far 'n do dh'fhiosraich mo chluasan-sa fuaim a' chiùil àird.

Bidh cuimhneachain taitnis ann an taisgeadh mo smuaintean
Mu d' òban tha cuartaichte le fuar-bheanntan àrd' —
Far 'n do ghrunnaich mi casruisgt' air beag airsteal no gruaman
B' fhada guilm na truaigh' anns an uair bho mo dhàil.

Mairead Chaimbeul

Nach fortanach fear chì le shùil
An tlachd tha 'n gnùis na h-ainnir
Tha tàmh an Uibhist ghorm nan stùc —
Tìr àghmhor ùire meala.

An t-eilean bòidheach muigh san iar
Far 'm miann leinn a bhith fantainn,
Far 'n cluinn sinn crònan a' Chuain Shiair
Tighinn iargaltach gu cladach.

Tha a cuailean dualach, dùthchas bòidhch',
Cur roinn na glòir' 'na pearsa;
Tha sìth tha deilbheadh bunait gràis
A' snàmh 'na dà shùil thlachdmhoir.

Bidh Sligh' Chloinn Uisn' air oidhche reòdht'
A' dòrtadh dòchais pailt dhomh
'S a' dealbhadh ìomhaigh na mnà òig'
Troimh dhuibhre neòil an airsneil.

Tha thu mar shoillseadh coinneil òir
Cur loinn air bòrd a' chaisteil,
A' lìonadh aitreabh mhór nan seud
Le fonn air ghleusadh aiteis.

Se còmhradh ciùin o d' ghrinn ròs-bheul
A stiùireadh creuchdan fad bhuam
Mar shéist a' chiùil tha siùbhlach réidh —
S tu iùl Deò-Ghréin' 'na taisbean.

Tha sunnd 'nad shaltairt air a' bhlàr
'S bidh fonn air sràid 'nad chascheum;
Tha furan taisgte riut o d' thùs
Mar ghàrradh fhlùr ùr-dhathte.

Cuairt a dh'Eilean na h-Òige

Ged a ghlac an aois mi
'S gach gaoid a tha 'na treòir,
'Nam measg gun tàinig caochlaidhean
Thug faochadh dha mo sheòrs':
Chan fheumainn ràimh no taoman
No gaoth a bhith 'nam sheòl
Gus m' aiseag thar a' chaolais
Gu eilean grinn na h-òig'.

Thug carbad chun na Lùdaig sinn
'S le sunnd chaidh sinn air bòrd
An eathair làidir lùthmhoir
Tha fo stiùireadh a' ghill' òig';
Nuair thug e chun an fhuaraidh i
'S a ghluais i mach bhon chòrs'
Bha 'n ataireachd fo gualainn
Dha mo chluasan-sa mar cheòl.

Ràinig sinne Éirisgeigh
Air feasgar réidh gun sgòth
'S gu h-aithghearr chaidh ar gàirdeachadh
Air càirdean sean is òg;
Ged bha mòran chuireadh fonn orm
'Nan cadal trom fon fhòd,
Le bàidh gun deach an cuimhneachadh
Nuair fhuair sinn cruinn mun bhòrd.

Tha seanfhacal ag innse dhuinn —
Is fìrinneach an sgeòil —
"Na cnuic cha dèan iad gluasad,
Ach coinnichidh sluagh sinn beò."

S tric bhios e 'na bhuannachd dhuinn
  Ar dualchas bhith mar as còir,
Is suim thoirt dha na subhailcean
  Tha fuaight' rinn bho ar n-òig'.

Chaith sinn oidhche chiatach ann
  Is bha gach sìon air dòigh:
Bha pailteas deoch is biadh againn
  Is sgeulachdan gu leòr;
Bha dannsaireachd is pìobaireachd
  Is rìbhinnean bu bhòidhch' —
'S nach sona thu, Dhòmhnaill Ruairidh,
  Bhon a bhuannaich thu bhean òg!

Màiri

Gun sgrìobh mi a' Ghàidhlig bhios bàidheil is fallain
  Mu bhòidhche na cailin as mais' ann an snuadh —
Chan fhiosrach leam aon té san t-saoghal air thalamh
  A dhùisgeadh fear ealain cho ealamh gu duan.

Taobh a' Chaolais rinn d' àrach gu tràth 'na do leanabh,
  Thug oiteag na mara dhut fallaineachd bhuan;
Chuireadh gàirich nan tonn thu gu trom 'na do chadal
  'S do dhùsgadh sa mhadainn cho fallain gun ghruaim.

Tha eachdraidh mun chaolas a dh'fhaodainn dhuibh aithris
  Mun t-saoghal chaidh seachad is gàbhaidhean cuain
Nuair bhiodh Ruairidh mac Nìll a' cur still á cuan Bharraigh
  'S a bhirlinn a' gearradh chìrean geala nan stuadh.

Ach tillidh mi 'n-dràst' a chur fàilt' air a' chailin,
  Na gorm shùilean meallaidh 's na mala gun ghruaim,
Na bilean as blàitheadh a tharraing a-steach anail
  Bhon tig còmhradh is caithream a tha taitneach do m' chluais.

Troigh chòmhnard air ùrlar gu sunndach le faram,
Do chalpannan geala chuireadh sradag 'nam bhuaidh;
Nas àille na flùr tha ùr-dhreach na h-ainnir,
'S tha caomh-ròs na madainn a' lasadh 'na gruaidh.

Tha h-ìomhaigh cho caoin-gheal ri faoileag na mara
A th' air faondrachd gach latha fo chathadh nan stuadh,
Mar ghrian dol don iar 's i triall ás ar sealladh
Sa chuan siar dol ga falach air ais air a cuairt.

Mo bheannachd gad ionnsaigh 's falbh thugad dùbailt'
Gu dùthaich nan dùbhghall a-null thar a' chuain
Bho dhùthaich na Gàidhlig far an òg fhuair thu d' àrach —
Far 'm bu tric 'na cheòl tàlaidh dhut gàirich a' chuain.

Na Solais Ùra

Ged tha geamhradh gruamach aognaidh
Eadar dùbhlachd agus faoilteach,
Tillidh earrach grinn le aoigheachd
'S cha bhi cuimhn' air gaoir na gaillinn.

Ged nach eil an gleann cho beòthail
'S a bha e ann an làithean m' òige,
Tha sradag ùr air tighinn 'nar dòchas
Gum bi ceòlraidh againn fhathast.

Thàinig solais ùr' 'nam fhianais
Le'n cuid boillsgidh a tha briagha:
Chì mi bhuam iad anns a' chiaradh
'S chì mi ciatach iad sa mhadainn.

Chì mi soillseach iad a' deàrrsadh
Mar reul-dhruidh a' tairgsinn fàilte,
Mar am fuaran anns an fhàsach
Don fhear phàiteach fad' bho chala.

Chan fhiosrach leam nì cho sunndach
No cho taitneach dha ar sùilean
Na bhith faicinn toit a' smùideadh
        Is solais ùra tighinn don bhaile.

Bidh Ceit Màiri agus Flòraidh
Cur nan cùirteanan an òrdagh:
Iad am-bliadhna dol air fògradh —
        Dol a chòmhnaidh dhan pholl chreadhaidh.

Thàinig Angela le ar dùrachd
'S thàinig Moira ann bho dhùthchas:
Thug iad soilleireachd as ùr dhuinn —
        Thug iad sunnd dhuinn agus aighear.

Mar a dh'Fhiosraich Mi Thu

Mar a dh'fhiosraich mi thu sann dh'inn's mi do chliù do chàch,
Se 'n gàire 'nad shùil teudan mo chiùil an àird.
Có nach ìobradh a smaoin do mhaise 's do dh'aoibh cho àrd?
'S leugh mise 'nad ghnùis nì nach dealaich gu'm mùch mo là.

Se mac-meanmna mo smuain le mànranachd aotrom réidh
Chuir mo long tron a' chaol le siùil gheal' agus gaoth 'na déidh;
Marbh-shruth bhith fo sròin gu marbhanta còmhnard sèimh —
A nì m' aiseag le sunnd gu m' acarsaid rùnach fhéin.

A' ghaoth tha triall thar a' chuain, thoir beannachdan bhuam a-null
Is aiseag mo sgeul le sealbh is deagh-ghean 'na cùl,
Air a liubhair le bàidh is guidhe cho blàth is rùn —
Lìonmhorachd ròs agus liosan nas bòidhche na ubhal.

Gach sòlas bhith snàmh mar eala air bhàrr nan stuadh,
Gach snas agus séist mar eunlaith nan speur gun ghruaim,
Mar shòbhrag nan allt bheir an t-earrach a-nall air chuairt —
No maighdeann na Tròidh a chur luingis air sheòl gu cuan.

Tha 'n t-acair sa ghrunnd air a' ghrinneal gu dlùth 's cha ghluais,
Chan eil feum air na siùil, tha iad paisgte dlùth gu cruaidh;
Thig gu deireadh gach cùis, tha chuibhle le sunnd dol mun cuairt
'S chì mise gu m' dheòin — mar a chunnaic — an ròs 'nad ghruaidh.

Mo Dhùrachd Thu Thilleadh

Mo dhùrachd thu thilleadh,
Mo dhùrachd thu thilleadh,
Mo dhùrachd thu thilleadh
    A-nall thar an t-sàil
Gu Uibhist nam fuaran
'S nan àrd-bheanntan gruamach —
An t-eilean beag uaine
    Tha cuartaicht' le sàl.

An t-eilean beag bòidheach
A dh'àraich 'nad òig' thu
Far an cluinneadh tu còisir
    Is crònan an làin
Is ceilearadh ceòlmhor
Na h-uiseig 's na smeòraich
A' cumail gach bròn bhuat
    'S cur sòlas 'nad phàirt.

Gu bheil sinn gad ionndrainn
On dh'fhàg thu an dùthaich
'S a sheòl thu, a rùin, bhuainn
    A-null thar an t-sàil:
Gach beannachd gad ionnsaigh
'S tu thilleadh gu sunndach
Gu Uibhist nan stùcan —
    Òg dhùthaich do ghràidh.

B'e samhladh don ròs thu
Á gàrradh nan neòinean,
B'e 'n driùchd far an fheòir thu
    San òg-mhadainn Mhàigh;

B'e 'm fuaran ri òl thu
Measg chluaintean na mòintich,
S tu 'n rìbhinn as bòidhche
        Chuir bròg air a sàil.

Bhon fhuair mi ort eòlas
'Nad mhàldaig bhig bhòidhich
Bha sìth agus sòlas
        'Nad òg-shùilean blàth;
Se deàrrsadh na gréine
San ùr-mhadainn chéitein
An dealbh nì mi fhéin dhiot,
        Òr-sheud nam bas bhàn.

Ròs na Mórchuis

Gur tu mo chéitean 's mo ghrian ag éirigh,
    Gur tu mo reul anns na speuran àrda;
Gur tu chairt-iùil leis an dèanainn cùrsa —
    S tu ailm mo stiùir 's is tu siùil mo bhàta.

S tu 'm flùr as bòidhche am measg nan ròsan,
    S tu 'm fuaran glòrmhor a dh'òlainn pàiteach;
S tu reul na h-oidhche a' deàrrsadh boillsgeach —
    S tu fhéin an daoimean chuir loinn air m' fhàinne.

S tu as gealach 's grian dhomh an speur na h-iarmailt,
    S tu ghaoth an-iar dhomh gu ciatach slàinteil;
S tu madainn bhòidheach 's an dealt air neòinein
    No feasgar glòrmhor 's na h-eòin cur fàilt' oirnn.

Mo bheatha s tù, seadh mo bhiadh is m' aodach,
    Mo bheachd, mo smaointinn, gach taobh an tàmh mi;
Mo chadal suaineach thu air mo chluasaig —
    Mo chombaist buan thu tro chuairt mo làithean.

A-cheart cho bòidheach ri Eilidh Thròidh thu
A chuir gu seòladh luing-mhór nan àrd-chrann;
Mar shneachd' nan cruachan tha cneas na gruagaich
No eal' nan stuadhan nuair b' uaisle shnàmh i.

Mar long a' seòladh, siùil ùr ga còmhdach,
Mar eilid bhòidheach measg ceò nan àrd-bheann;
Mar shòbhraig samhraidh air bruaich an alltain
No smeòrach ghreannmhor sa ghleann cur fàilt' oirnn.

Nuair thig an geamhradh le stoirm is anntlachd
Bidh gruaim is greann air gach gleann is fàsach;
Se 'n deàrrsadh sunndach a tha 'nad shùilean
A chuireadh dùdlachd gun diù fo m' shàilean.

Mo bheannachd buan leat gach taobh an gluais thu,
A rìbhinn uasal nam buadhan sònraicht',
'S ged s fhada bhuam thu bidh thu 'nam bhruadair —
'S gur tric mo smuaintean dol cuairt a Leòdhas.

Taobh Deas Loch Baghasdail

Taobh Deas Loch Baghasdail nan stùc
'S nan glaicean flùrach bòidheach,
Am fasgadh Éiseabhal nan gleann,
'S nan easan cam 's nam frògan,
Far an cluinn thu gaoir nan allt
A' ruith 'nan deann tron mhòintich
'S far an cluinn thu gaoir nan eun
Mun éirich grian na glòir ann.

Far an cluinn thu gàir a' chuain
A' slapraich cruaidh san òban
'S onfhadh gaoithe feadh nan cluan
Is seillean ruadh a' crònan;
Far am faic thu lach a' snàmh,
I fhéin 's a h-àl ga steòrnadh,
Far 'm faic thu canach feadh nan stùc
Cur brat geal ùr air mòintich.

Chì thu bàtaichean air cuan
'S fir thapaidh chruaidh gan seòladh,
Nach gabh geilt o stoirm on tuath
Le gailleann chruaidh gun tròcair;
Ged a dh'atadh muir 'na glinn
Is marcachd-sìn' mar chòp-eas',
Gu ruig iad leatha cala slàn
Á stàirneil a' chuain chròicich.

'N àm éirigh grian sa mhadainn thràth
Bidh dealt air bhàrr nan neòinean:
Gach nì cho nàdarra mun cuairt
Le lusan snuadhmhor òrbhuidh;
An ceò a' còmhdach bàrr nam beann
Is ùrlar gleann na mòintich
Is ceilearadh aig eòin nan speur,
A' cur air ghleus an ceòlraidh.

Gur inntinneach bhith ann a' tàmh
Fo bhonn is sgàil nan ceò-bheann:
Ged shéideadh i le stoirm on iar
Tha fasgadh 's dìon gu leòr ann;
Chan eil éis air neach a th' ann,
Tha annlan de gach seòrs' ann,
Tha sìth is sonas feadh nam bruach —
'S gur mór an luach seach òr e.

Orasaigh

Air iomall fiadhaich de cheann an iardheas
A dh'Uibhist ghrianach mu'n iadh an sàile
Tha 'n t-eilean ianach nan creagan ciar-chas
An nàbachd crìoch ri Cuan Siar nan gàir-thonn.

Ged bhios Neiptiun a' maoimeadh daonnan,
Cha d' chuir e gaoid 'na do chaol-dhruim làidir —
Sheas thu suas ri gach fairge bhaoghail
A bhrist ri d' aodann le faochainn thàireil.

Nam biodh na daoine a threabh gach taobh dhiot
'S a dh'fhiosraich gaoid ann an saothair beòshlaint
Fad oidhche geamhraidh mun chagailt céilidh
Gur mì a dh'éisteadh ri sgeul an còmhraidh.

Tha lorg an t-sealgair gu pailt ri cunntadh
Measg chreagan ùdlaidh aig tiùrr do chòrsa —
Is iomadh diùnlaoch le ghunna dùbailt'
A choisich sunndach a-null an dòirlinn.

Nan d'fhuair thu tàlann gu bruidhinn Gàidhlig
Bhiodh eachdraidh chàirdeil le bàidh 'nad chòmhradh;
Gur pailt an t-Hàllann tha ùir is cnàmhan
Nam fuireann làidir bha snàmh mu d' òban.

Tha tràigh de ghainmhich air dhath an airgid
Is bàigh tha ainmeil le dealbhach' bòidhche;
Do mhullach cruthail air chumadh dùn-lios
Fo chuibhrig fhlùran 's an driùchd gan òradh.

An àm an t-samhraidh bidh crònan tìoma
Aig toiseach lìonaidh a' tighinn gu d' chòrsa,
'S an àm a' gheamhraidh aig toiseach tràghaidh
Bidh nuallain làstail aig gairge bhòc-thonn.

Ri stoirm an fhaoiltich bidh 'n fhairg' 'na taom-bhoil
A' gleacadh faobhair ri d' aodann gròbach;
A dh'olc na dh'éiginn cha d'rinn thu géilleadh,
'S cha d' ghluais do stéidh ri séideadh Aeòlus.

Tha ealtainn sgèimheach mu d' sgorran iom-sgoilt',
Thu dhaibh 'nad dhìon-àit' bho shìontan fògairt;
Bidh ròn gu h-uallach air bhàrr nan stuadh-ghlas —
Tha 'n tìr 's an cuan ann an dual a bheò-bhith.

Bheir àm h-Éill Pàdraig dhut trusgan àraidh,
Bidh brat de bhlàthan 'nan àill gad chòmhdach
Bidh ceòl na cuaiche ga mheasg ri suaimhneachd,
Is thig luchd cuairt thar a' chuain gad fheòrachd.

Sgòrr an Fhéidh

Ri aodainn bhuirbe nan sìontan agus fiadhaichead a' chuain,
Ri séideadh greannach iorgailleach bhon ear 's bhon iar is tuath
Tha stéidh do bhuinn 'na eilich mar chàrnaich iarainn chruaidh —
'S cha dèan an stoirm le dhìorras do dhìocail san droch uair.

Chan eil thu ann ad' ònrachdan 's cha laigh ort bròn no gruaim,
Bidh fairge Rubh' na h-Òrdaig a' còmhradh riut gach uair;
'S ged s tric a bhios i còmhstri riut 's a' gròbadh air do ghruaidh,
Tha companais bho'r n-òig' agaibh le deòin a chum sibh suas.

Tha naidheachdan gu leòr agad nam b' deòin leat bhith gan inns':
Is iomadh neach chuir eòlas ort tha 'n-diugh fon fhòd sa chill
A dhìreadh suas ri d' chliathaichean 's nach cromadh sìos le sgìths —
Se tapachd thug bhon iargain iad 's gum b' dèanadach teachd an tìr.

Ged as gruamach aognaidh thu san fhaoilteach ghreannach fhuar,
Bheir an samhradh caochladh ort is aoigheachd air do shnuadh —
Fàsaidh cluaran frioghach ort is frith-raineach nam bruach
'S bidh mac-tall' air madainn chéitein freagairt sgèimheil ceòl na cuaich'.

Ged as fad' bhon dh'fhalbh an òige bhuat cha d' laigh ort bròn no smùr,
Chum thu inntinn bheothachail 's cha tig na deòir bho d' shùil;
Chum thu beachd is mheòmhraich thu gu sònraicht' air gach iùil —
'S cha mhiannaich thu bhith stòrasach no càrnadh òir air chùl.

Nuair thig dorchadas na h-oidhche ort chan oilltich thu tro fhuath,
Chan fheum thu solas coinnle gu bhith boillsgeadh ort mun cuairt;
Cha chuireadh gaisreadh shaighdearan bho d' oighreachd thu air ruaig —
Gur daingeann air do stéidhean thu de dh'eilich chàrnaich chruaidh.

Tha seallaidhean tha sònraichte ri aimsir shoininn chiùin
Ri am faicinn bho do ghròbain tha sòlasach don t-sùil:
Chithear long a' seòladh le fear eòlach aig an stiùir —
Am maraidheachd nan cròic-thonnan 'na òige chuir e ùidh.

Is iomadh fleasgach umhail is maighdeann chiùin nam beus
Dh'fhàg cladaichean an dùthchais dol a-null gu tìrean céin'
A chrath an làmh le dùrachd 's iad ag amharc dlùth 'nan déidh —
'S na deòir 'nan sruth le'n sùilean a' cur cùl ri Sgòrr an Fhéidh.

Siubhal Chluaintean

Tha iomadh suaimhneas am measg nan cluan seo
Nuair théid thu cuairt feadh nan uain'-chnoc bòidheach:
Gach lus cho ùrail fo dhriùchd an t-samhraidh
'S gun chuimhn' air geamhradh no àm na reòdht-ghaoith'.

Gach nì cho àghmhor le sìth is sàmhchair
Measg ghlinn is àilean is shrathan còmhnard;
Am fraoch 'na loinn ann an soills' na gréine
Cur sunnd 'nad cheum siubhal sléibh nan ceò-bheann.

Bidh crònan caochain le ealaidh caoinis
Mar thàladh gaoil bilean caomh na h-òlachd
A' stiùireadh d' inntinn gu tìr na réite
'S a' cur 'nad dhéidh tuailis eud an-dòchais.

Tha fóghnadh rìomhaidh am measg nam frìth seo
Le roghainn dhìthean tha cinntinn òrail;
Tha 'n cluaran-deilgneach 'na shuaithneas prìseil
'S an t-sòbhrag ghrinn taobh an uillt cho glòrmhor.

Ged nach eil àros no daoine tàmh ann
Bha uair bha càirdeas is bàidh sna ceò-ghlinn,
Bhiodh fuaim a' chàrd' anns a h-uile fàrdaich
'S bhiodh saothair bhrà bleith nan grànlach eòrna.

Bhiodh càradh lìon ann le eòlas iasgair
'S bhiodh cuidheall-shnìomha gu dian ri crònan;
Bhiodh buillean làidir gan toirt air spàl ann
'S bhiodh mnathan làmhchair a' luadh nan clòithean.

Biodh aoibh is bàidh air an aodainn chàirdeil
Measg sìochaint sàmhchair am bràigh nam mòinteach,
'S ged dhìobair foghlam dhiubh tiodhlaic chungaidh
Bu deàrrsant' cliùmhor bha iùil an eòlais.

Bha 'm beatha làitheil a' triall neo-eudach
Bho mhochthrath éirigh gu réis na glòmainn;
Cha robh beairteas no stòr 'nan ùidh-san —
Ach dhùin an sùilean an dùil ri sòlas.

'N àm éirigh gréine thar slios nan cruadhlach
Cur gathan snuadhmhor mun cuairt na mòintich
Cur sgàil na h-oidhche 'na dheann air chùlaibh
'S a' toirt madainn ùr dhuinn le sùgradh dòchais.

Ged duaichnidh eugnaidh a dhreach san fhaoilteach
Bheir samhradh caochladh le chaomh-chruth òrail
Bidh eòin na h-àirde cur mìle fàilt' air
Le roinn is dàin ann am blàths na ceòlraidh.

Glaic Ruairidh

O fàilt', a ghlaic as dreachmhor snuadh
Far 'n d' ghluais mi 'n làithean m' òig',
Far 'n robh mi leum air feadh nam bruach
Gun ghruaman no gun bhròn;
Am measg an fhraoich air aodann bheann
Is ghleann mu'n iath an ceò,
Far 'n cluinnear monmhair bhinn nan allt
Cur steall air feadh nam fròg.

O, siud na làithean a bha saor
'S a bhios 'nam smaoin ri m' bheò
An uair bha m' inntinn réidh gun daors'
Mar naosg air feadh an fheòir;

Mus do dh'fhiosraich mi gach gaoid
    Bhios daonnan a' tighinn òirnn
'S mus tàinig coimhicheas an t-saoghail
    Le thuiltean gaoir 'nam chòir.

Gur sgapt' an-diugh air feadh gach taoibh
    An comann aoigheil còir
A b' àbhaist bhith cluich air feadh an fhraoich
    Cho aotrom ris na h-eòin —
Tha cuid 'nan suain san dachaigh bhuain
    Fo ghlasan fuar nam bòrd
Nach till air ais gu bràch air chuairt
    Do ghleannan uain' nan còs.

An uair thig mìos na Bealltainn Màigh
    Gur àghmhor bhios gach flùr
Air feadh nan glaic a' teachd ri fàs
    Gar gàirdeachas le sunnd;
Bidh lusan maoth air feadh nan cluan
    Cho òrail snuadh fo dhriùchd,
Is còisridh ghrinn nam measgadh teud
    A' gleusadh a cruit-chiùil.

Bidh biolair uain' as bòidhche snuadh
    A' fàs mun cuairt nan lòn,
Bidh dail-chuach eireachd, seud nam bruach,
    'Na shuaithneas measg an fheòir;
Gach lus bheir beòshlàint dha do smaoin
    Air feadh gach taoibh 'nan glòir —
An t-sòbhrag 's frith-raineach nan cluan,
    'S 'nam measg bidh 'n cluaran òir.

Gur tric a théid mi mach air chuairt
    'S a bheir mi ruaig mun chrò —
Bidh na cnuic 's na tomain uain'
    Ag ath-nuadhachadh dhomh m' òig'
'S a' toirt air ais nan làithean saor'
    'S na faoineasan gun ghò
Is cleachdaidhean an òg-ghnàiths fhaoin
    A dh'fhalbh mar sgaoileas ceò.

Sgrìobhaidh Mi le Dùrachd mu Rùn na Té Òig Seo

Sgrìobhaidh mi le dùrachd mu rùn na té òig seo,
Chan fhaca mi san dùthaich am flùr as bòidhche,
Sgrìobhaidh mi le dùrachd mu rùn na té òig seo.

An Uibhist ghorm nan àrd-bheanntan
A thogadh suas an t-àilleagan —
Rìbhinn ghrinn nam blàth-shùilean a thug an àird mo chòmhradh.

Eilean gorm nan àrd-bheanntan,
Bidh daonnan fuinn na Gàidhlig ann
Cho fads bhios tuinn an t-sàile tighinn le gàir-gheal chun a' chòrsa.

Sgrìobhaidh mi san uair seo dhuibh
Mu 'bòidhchead 's a snuadhmhoire —
Tha falt dubh clannach dualach sìos mu guaillinnean ga còmhdach.

Tha fiamh a gàir' cho inntinneach
Ri còisir-chiùil nam frìthean
Nuair thig an samhradh dìtheanach air ais gu Tìr an Eòrna.

Gur gile leam an deud aice
Na sneachd' air mullach Éiseabhail
Nuair thig am faoilteach beucach le chuid ghéirid rinn a chòmhraig.

Tha aoighealachd ga cuartachadh
'S i càirdeil bàidheil uallachais —
Tha dearbhadh ann a gluasad gu bheil buaidhean aic' tha sònraicht'.

Tha mil nam flùr a' tàrmachadh
'Na h-ìomhaigh aoigheil bhlàth-chridheach —
Cho rìomhach ann ri màldaig a chuir m'a sàiltean brògan.

Tha h-anail air a cùbhrachadh
Le measgachadh de chungaidhean:
Cha cheannaich òr am bùthan iad — bho dhùthchas thig an seòrsa.

Mo dhùrachd théid an-dràst' 'uic',
Mo dhòchas gura làidir e
Gun dèan am freastal fàbhar rium a-màireach bhith 'na còmhair.

Cuairt Dhòmhnaill Iain feadh nan Gleann

Thug mi chuairt feadh nan cluaintean bòidheach,
Na glinn 's na h-uain'-chnuic tha smuadhmhor còmhdaicht',
A-mach Glaic Ruairidh 's mu chuairt na Sròine
Gu Meall nam Bùthan 's a-null na h-òban.

Na Creagan Gorm' agus Meall an Iasgaich
Nan sealladh àghmhor fo bhlàthan briagha:
Sgòrr an Fhéidh ann fo reubadh shìontan
'S e giùlain cleòca de cheò na h-iarmailt'.

Tha Rubh' na h-Òrdaig 'na charraig ùdlaidh
A' cumail còmhstri ri dòrnadh dhùilean:
Na creagan cruaidh' aig a' chuan ga sgùradh
Le doineann throm tighinn á com nam brùchd-thonn.

Ged s corrach cas Glaic an Daimh ri dìreadh,
Tha sealladh àghmhor bho bhàrr a cìrein;
Bidh fonn neo-bhruaillein a' gluasad d' inntinn
A' cluinntinn uainneart is buaireas strìtheil.

Tha monmhair aibhne a' ruith troimh Gharbh-Shlios
Mar cheòlraidh dhrùidhteach is ciùineachd seanchais,
Mar dhoimhne aoibhneachd air aodann leanabain
'S mar dhriùchd a' crùnadh nam flùr san anmoch.

Tha Gleann Gorm agus Glaic a' Chìobair
Mar bha iad riamh bho chian nan linntean
Gu fàsgadh tèaraint' ri sìontan millteach —
'S bidh chaora bhàn faighinn sgàil bhon dìl' ann.

Tha Rubh' a' Mhoil far am pailt an eunlaith
Cur mìle fàilt' ort le bàidh is ciatachd;
Bidh 'n fhaoileag bhàn tric a' snàmh gun fhiamhlachd,
A' sireadh beòshlaint m'a chòrs' ag iasgach.

Far mo chuairt feadh nam bruach gun thill mi
Gu cadal suaineach air cluasaig mhìn-gheal;
Rinn mi dùsgadh le sunnd 's toil-inntinn
'S fhuair mi peann 's mar a bh' ann gun sgrìobh mi.

Ina

Gur e mis' a th' air mo dhòigh —
  Ghabh Rìgh na Glòrach truas rium
An uair a fhuair mi Rìbhinn Bhàn
  A chumas blàth bhon fhuachd mi.

Anns a' mhadainn nì i tea
  'S gun sgrìob i mach an luath dhomh,
Glanaidh i dhomh pìob an stòbh —
  Gach sìon air dòigh mun gluais mi.

Deasaichidh i biadh air bòrd,
  Brot is feòil mar as dualach;
Aig deireadh seachdain gheibh sinn iasg,
  Is botal fìon air uairean.

Tha gach cùis a' tighinn ri m' chàil,
  Rinn cuibhl' an fhàbhair gluasad —
Pension agus *scratch card*
  Is rìbhinn bhàn air cluasaig.

Mìle marbhphaisg air bhith faoin,
  Tha iomadh gaoid 'na ghluasad;
Na chuir mi shìol an làithean m' òig'
  Bhiodh coirce 's eòrn' gam buain leam.

Taigh Sgoile Glaic Ruairidh

Gluais, a chlàrsach, 's dèan dùsgadh
(S ro fhad' tha thu san dùiseal)
'S cuir teudan a' chiùil ann an òrdagh
'S cuir air sgéithe an duan seo
'S mi dol a-mach 'na mo smuaintean
Am measg fraoch geugagach snuadhmhor na mòintich.

Mo mhac-mheanmna air gluasad
A-mach gu iomall Glaic Ruairidh
Far an tric robh mi cluaineas 'nam òige
Feadh nan cas-thoman uaine
Air an còmhdach le luachair
Far bheil fìoruisg' an fhuarain a' còpadh.

Far bheil nuallan nan steud-shruth
A' tighinn a-nuas troimh na féithean
Air an ruamhar aig reubadh nan còp-eas,
Air an stialladh 'nam pìosan
Aig tuiltean 's aig dìle
A' dol air ais ann an tìm gu àm Nòah.

Bidh na tuiltean 'nam fiadhaiche
A' tighinn a-nuas le na cliathaichean
Aig bearraidhean riabhach nan ceò-bheann,
A' tionndadh 's a' fiaradh
Troimh chuislean is bhlianagan
Gus an ruig iad bial Bàgh Marulaig.

Sann fo iomall nam fuar-bheann
Is fasgadh na tuath-ghaoith'
A bha taigh-sgoile Glaic Ruairidh 'na òrdagh
Air làrach bheag uaine
Le fraoch air a chuartachadh
Far am fàsadh an cluaran bu bhòidhche.

Siud an òigridh bha fonnmhor
A' ruith 's a' leum feadh nan tom ud,
A' grunnachadh troimh pholl is troimh chòinnich,
A-muigh air aodann nam fìreach
Ged bhiodh a' ghailleann 's an dìl' ann —
Cha robh iomradh san tìm ud air brògan.

Cha robh ar n-éideadh ro phrìseil,
Cha do dh'fhiosraich sinn sìoda,
Cha robh seudan an rìomhaidh gar còmhdach —
Cha d'fhuair sinn mar dhìleab
Ach cruaidh-chàs na h-ìsle
A chum fodha san dìg sinn gu'r srònan.

Ged bu luideach a bhà sinn
Ann an aimsir an ànraidh
Chuir eu-treòir nan càs sinn air fògairt —
Chaidh cuid dhinn gu sàile
Gu ruigheachd ionadan àraid
Air drochaidean àrd' luingis seòlaidh.

Ann an doimhneachd mo smuaintean
'S ann am breislich mo bhruadair
Bidh mo chéilidh a' gluasad an còmhnaidh
A-mach gu iomall nan cruadhlach
Gu seunachd Glaic Ruairidh
Far bheil cuimhneachain bhuan dhomh air m' òige.

Dàin Eile / Other Poems

Of the following 79 other poems by Dòmhnall Aonghais Bhàin, some are referred to in the Introduction; most appeared in *The Stornoway Gazette* or *Am Pàipear,* while other sources are specified below. In each case the title is given followed by the first line.

'A Rìbhinn Bhòidheach Shìobhalta': A rìbhinn bhòidheach shìobhalta.
'A' Bheinn': Nan robh thu briathrach le teanga thìoma.
'A' Mhaighdeann Chriadhadh': Sann madainn Di-Dòmhnaich a chunnaic mi 'n ògbhean. *An Tuil* p. 512.
'A-Muigh air Iomall nan Cuantan': A-muigh air iomall nan cuantan.
'A-Muigh san Iar': A-muigh san iar am meadhoin cuain.
'Air Bruaich an Uillt': Nuair sheasas mi air bruaich an uillt.
'Air Chuairt an Cille Bhrìghde': Bhon a thug mi 'n sgrìob seo a chluaintean Chille Bhrìghde.
'An Iolaire': Shuas gu h-àrd san iarmailt.
'An Rìbhinn Bhòidheach': Nas àille na flùr tha fo dhriùchd anns an Ògmhios.
'An t-Allt': Le monmhair bhinn.
'An t-Eilean Àghmhor Bòidheach': Gun sgrìobh mi sìos a-nis an dàn.
'An t-Sòbhrag': A shòbhrag dhreach-bhuidh' grinn nam bruach.
'An Té Bhàn': Ged tha m' òige fada null.
'Away in the West': Away in the West in the turbulent ocean.
'Bana-Charaid': Se eilean Uibhist nan stùcan far an dlùth fàs an eòrna.
'Bean na Buana': S cridheil sunndach i 'na gluasad.
'Beanntan mo Dhùthcha': Gur bòidheach is greannmhor.
'Bha Uair a Dhèanainn Sùgradh': Bha uair a dhèanainn sùgradh.
'Bhon a dh'Imrich an Geamhradh': Bhon a dh'imrich an geamhradh.
'Bhon dh'Fhalbh Uainn an Dùbhlachd': Bhon dh'fhalbh uainn an Dùbhlachd is aimsir na dùire.
'Caileag Òg': Cha d' dheàrrs a' ghrian san tràth-mhadainn nas blàthmhoir' na do bhòidhch'.
'Caochladh Tìde': Nuair a dh'fhalbhas am faoilteach le chuid faobhair is fuachd.
'Catrìona': Ri taobh a' chuain chaidh d' àrach suas. *Gairm* 119 p. 240; *Voice of the Bard* p. 9.
'Chì Mi Thu': Chì mi thu mar long air sàl.
'Cho Grinn 's a Tharraing Anail': Gun glac mi peann gu teann 'nam làimh.
'Cluaintean mo Ghaoil': A chluaintean mo ghaoil gura caomh leam ur bruachan.
'Cumha don Rìbhinn': Ged a dh'fhàg sinn san ùir thu ann an dubhadh a' bhàis.
'Daphne': A rìbhinn bhòidheach a' chùil dhuinn. *Gairm* 119 p. 241.
'Dealbh Essie Stiùbhairt': An leabhar-eachdraidh an luchd-cuairte. *Gairm* 183 p. 277.
'Don Uiseig': Fàilt' a spiorad aoibhneis.
'Dreach an Fhraoich': Gur briagha dreachmhor dath an fhraoich.
'Dùrachd': Gach àm dhen bhliadhna mo mhìle dùrachd.
'Ealasaid': Gur bòidhche leam na flùr thu.
'Eilean Àghmhor nam Buadh': Eilean àghmhor nam buadh 'na laigh' anns a' chuan.
'Eilean Beag Uibhist': Se eilean beag Uibhist 'na laigh' anns a' chuan.
'Eilean nan Crà-Ghèadh': Se eilean nan crà-ghèadh. *Gairm* 184 p. 324.
'Eilein Uibhist Ghorm nan Cluaintean': Eilein Uibhist ghorm nan cluaintean.
'Fàilt' air an Earrach': Fàilt' air an earrach tighinn gu fearann ar dùthchais.

'Fàilt' air an Rìbhinn': Fàilt' air an rìbhinn thàinig mìltean thar chuan.
'Fàilt' Ort a-Nall thar an Aisig': Fàilt' ort a-nall thar an aisig.
'Fàilte Angela': Fàilte ort fhéin, a rìbhinn òg.
'Fàilte Ann Marie gu Taobh a-Deas Loch Bhaghasdail': Sgrìobhaidh mi mun rìbhinn seo tha tàmh an Tìr an Eòrn'. Four verses have been published as 'Màiri Anna Chaimbeul': Fàilt' ort fhéin a Rìbhinn òg, gur bòidheach rinn thu fàs.
'Fàilte Hannah': Mìle fàilt' ort a' tighinn thar sàile.
'Fàilte Linda': Mìle fàilte don rìbhinn bhòidhich.
'Fàilte Moira': A rìbhinn òg rinn tighinn a-nall.
'Feasgar Samhraidh': Feasgar samhraidh geal ciatach'. *Gairm* 151 p. 208.
'Fraoch a' Bhadain': Fraoch a' bhadain uaine tha 'n tìr mo luaidh a' fàs. *Gairm* 118 p. 173, *The Scotsman* 27 August 1983.
'Ged a Gheibhinn Gach Stòr': Ged a gheibhinn gach stòr agus taisealadh maoin.
'Ged Shéideadh a' Ghailleann san Fhaoilteach': Ged shéideadh a' ghailleann san fhaoilteach.
'Gleann na Ceòlraidh 'nam Òige 's 'nam Aois': Sann an gleann na ceòlraidh.
'Griomsaigh': O eilean àghmhor an taic an t-sàile. *Gairm* 120 p. 376.
'Gur Àghmhor a' Chruinneag': Gur àghmhor a' chruinneag.
'Haunts of my Childhood': Haunts of my childhood distinguished in story.
'Madainn Samhraidh': S bòidheach madainn samhraidh ann an gleann nan ròs.
'Maighdeann Bhòidheach Chàirinis': Si maighdeann bhòidheach Chàirinis.
'Maighdeann Loch a' Mhuilinn': Nam biodh mo long fo h-éideadh. *Voice of the Bard* p. 21.
'Maighdeann nan Òr-Chleachda': Mar as mò théid de dh'ùine ri cunntais do réis.
'Maighdeann Òg': Ged rugadh anns a' gheamhradh mi ri aimsir aingealt' fhuar.
'Màiri an Fhuilt Dhualaich': Gun sgrìobh mi fhìn an dàn seo dhuibh.
'Marbhrann do Choinneach Mac a' Choisiche á Dalabrog': Nuair bha dùil againn ri sùgradh 's a' bhliadhna ùr a' dol thighinn oirnn.
'Mìle Beannachd aig a' Chaileig': Mìle beannachd aig a' chaileig.
'Mìle Fàilt' agus Buaidh Dhut': Mìle fàilt' agus buaidh dhut.
'Mo Mhac-Meanma 's mo Pheann air Chuairt': Glacaidh mi 'nam mheòirean thu le sòlas agus uaill.
'Moladh Mnathan-Eiridinn Ospadal an Rathaig Mhóir, Inbhir Nis': Bhon fhuair mi léirsinn is fradharc ùr. *Gairm* 171 p. 208, *An Tuil* p. 510.
'Na Glaicean Uaine': Na glaicean uaine fo fhraoch is luachair.
'Ri Iomall na Fairge': Ri iomall na fairge far bheil garbhaich a' chuain.
'Rìbhinn an t-Sùgraidh': Rìbhinn an t-sùgraidh 's na gnùis chridheil bhlàith.
'Rìbhinn Dhonn nan Dual': A dh'ainneoin fuachd nan dùilinn.
'Rìbhinn Òg a' Chùil Bhuidhe': A rìbhinn òg a' chùil bhuidhe, mìle fàilt' ort a dh'Uibhist nan stùc.
'S Bòidhche t' Ìomhaigh na Ghrian ag Éirigh': S bòidhche t' ìomhaigh na ghrian ag éirigh.
'She Sat Down Beside Me': She sat down beside me.
'Si Òg-Mhadainn Shamhraidh an Samhla dha d' Bhòidhche': Si òg-mhadainn shamhraidh an samhla dha d' bhòidhche.
'Sìth': Sìth an aoibhnis tha loinn 'na h-òrdagh.
'The Rose of Canniesburn Hospital': Far away o'er the sea where the pine trees does grow.
'Though the Winter is Raging upon Us': Though the winter is raging upon us.
'Tighinn an t-Samhraidh': Tha 'n samhradh grinn air tighinn mun cuairt.
'Uibhist nan Stùcan': Uibhist nan stùcan a-muigh anns an iar.
'Uibhist': Eilean àlainn nan stùcan. *Gairm* 120 p. 374.
'Ùrachadh': Tha 'n aimsir ghreannach reòthta a' toirt òirnne sgleò na truaigh'.